Jack in the Pulpit

Jack in the Pulpit

memories of a country parson

Illustrated by Henry Brewis

Bridge Studios
Morpeth
Northumberland
1987

First published in Great Britain in 1987

by Bridge Studios,
   4B Bridge Street,
   Morpeth,
   Northumberland,
   NE61 1NB.

   Tel.: 0670 518101/519561

ISBN 0 9512630 0 5

Reprint 1987
Reprint 1987
Reprint 1988

Typeset and printed in Great Britain by J. Catherall & Co.
(Printers) Ltd., at the Abbey Press, Commercial Place,
Priestpopple, Hexham, Northumberland.

Jack in the Pulpit

Reverend John Richardson, better known as Jack, was educated at St Aidan's Theological College, Cheshire and ordained in Durham Cathedral in 1948. In his ministry he served both at sea and in country parishes. Before ordination he was in the Royal Navy, his first ship being HMS *Hood*.

He then served in the R.N. as a chaplain and is proud of the fact that he had a watchkeeping certificate for both navigation and engineering and was also a 'sin bosun' — the term for a naval padre.

After leaving the Royal Navy he worked for the Missions to Seamen and was also Senior Chaplain, R.N.R. His parishes were all in the north east of England — Wearside, Teesside and Northumberland. He was also Chaplain to the Earl of Durham.

In 1970 he was awarded the O.B.E. for services to the Royal Navy.

Now retired, he is busier than ever and lives at Blagdon in Northumberland.

Foreword

When my daughter Christine was a small girl, she brought home, at the end of a school term, a book with a soft paper cover and lots of grubby finger marks indicating the amount of industry put into the enclosed pages. The front cover bore a prominent but irregular legend which read 'My News Book'. Its contents formed a kind of diary. Whenever anything that was considered by her to be news occurred, my daughter entered it into her book, graphically detailing the items with grotesque drawings. To the adult mind there was much happy entertainment in its reading, but to her much more serious mind every entry was of tremendous import. For instance, the family might have gone on a car ride to visit the town of the Immortal Bard and, having seen all the relics, cottages and places appertaining to his glorious memory, my daughter would write, 'Went out in the car and saw a robin redbreast'. Alongside would appear a drawing of a red breasted ostrich, under which would be written the identity, 'A Robin', and the Bard would be noticed by her perceiving parents through the complete lack of reference to him. The little girl was so right. She was young and full of life and vigour, appreciative of life, light and colour. A man, full dead for countless years, had no place in her six years maturity.

She may weep for a bird found dead in the garden but through her tears she would see the gay fluttering of a butterfly, or the scarlet dash of the peony and she would be back once more with things that were living and moving. Her 'news' was dynamic because it had to do with life. Her world was so real and filled with adventure because of the life which cascaded ceaselessly before her wondering and surprised eyes.

In this book I have tried to emulate the simple yet profound workings of Christine's mind. I will unfold those things which I found fascinating and full of life although I know that there was a deeper and more profound side to my ministry. While my stories may be entertaining and lighthearted, they truly happened and in them we see truths which really matter to the average family in the home.

I have at this moment gazed meditatively through the window and my attention was drawn to the giant red ball that seems to hesitate in the sky as if reluctant to say 'goodnight'. The darkening shadows beneath the garden fence escaped me but I noticed a thrush sitting on my spade handle. Not being a little girl I did not thrill at the sight of the songster but made a mental note that my spade must be brought in before darkness claims the scene and obliterates my spade from existence until tomorrow's slanting rays of dawn resurrects it. 'Unless ye become as little children'. With childlike delight I have written my 'News Book' and have endeavoured to keep the stories simple, pithy and dynamic. Real life is not made up of big things, but to those who have eyes to see, and a twinkle in those eyes, it is the bundle of small things that create our records.

The pages I have written here are not in any way an autobiography. They record parochial memories. I have other memoirs yet to compose; those of my naval days, but I hope that they will form another book. I feel that it would be interesting as I served in two vastly differing roles, that of an engineer officer and later as a Chaplain, R.N.

I hope that all readers of this book enjoy it as much as I have enjoyed writing it.

John Richardson (Jack)

Chester-le-Street

Good timing

The unyielding new boots of the bridegroom's father refused to co-ordinate with the excess of alcohol in his blood and he fell down the vestry steps. The bride's father looked at the prostrate figure with what might have been disgust but more probably envy. Upon my looking at the puritanic stiffness of the bride's mother my guess was that it was envy. The groomsman, accompanying a willow-thin bridesmaid, wore a toupee which lay rather out of trim causing an optical effect of a zig-zag parting in his hair. Maybe I was envious too for my parting is as wide as a motorway. It also seemed as if some of his father's beverages had spilled over to the bridegroom who seemed to have only a detached interest in the proceedings. His slurred 'I will' was so indistinct that I had to demand that he repeat it. The bride appeared to have her huge bouquet of red roses glued to her fingers for she even managed to sign the marriage register without relinquishing the impeding blooms. The best man seemed to be the organiser producing the fees to the exact penny and the ring at the correct moment. It was a pity that the ring refused the hurdle of the bride's knuckle and, despite advice to spit on it, remained there, as at half mast, for the rest of the service. There is an unwritten law among clergy that invitations to wedding receptions should be refused if given verbally in the vestry at the conclusion of the service. If a couple or their families truly desire the company of the clergy at the reception they will include them in their mailing list. However, rules are made to be broken especially if the curate's wife is shopping in a distant town and has left her

1

spouse to fend for himself. So, having had a boiled egg and coffee for lunch I was pleased to accept the bride's mother's invitation.

Above the baker's shop was a large upper room suitable for wedding receptions, leek shows and jumble sales. Oddly enough it was occasionally used by the Marriage Guidance Council and the Samaritans. By the time I had cleared up the vestry, deposited the registers and fees in the safe and had divested myself of my surplice, retaining my cassock which effectively covered my tattered grey flannels, I brought up the stern of a line of guests still waiting to be officially received by the bridal party. I was halfway up the stairway and the smell of bread and sticky buns by-passed the downward stench of pease pudding and cooked ham. Proceedings seemed to have been suspended, for after almost a quarter of an hour I had not made any progress and was thinking of going home. Then the deadlock was broken by a piercing cry.

'Make way for the bride; she has started her labour pains!' Obligingly we flattened ourselves against the wall to afford an easier passage for the bride as she jerked her way downward accompanied by the imminent grandmother. The red roses, still held in one hand, drooped downwards while the other hand clenched and unclenched with each spasm.

'Good luck' the guests wished her but did not yield the priority of their positions in the queue.

Suddenly we were in the room. At the top table stood, in silent eloquence, a vacant chair. I was placed near to the door and opposite to a middle aged woman who educated me on the difficulties of childbirth. She had experienced its attendant dangers and perils eight times, so my meal remained mainly untouched as my stomach rebelled. The bridegroom looked a little bewildered and was no doubt congratulating himself on his excellent timing.

Occasionally a guest would quip,

'Cheer up, lad; we've never lost a father yet,' or

'Get his name down for a house straightaway.'

About half past five and after the groom had cut the cake one of the guests returned from the street below with a pink newspaper.

'Right lads, let's have you.'

Standing in the middle of the floor he began to read out the final football results while the men checked their pools coupons. Despite the fact that these coupons had been in church it would appear that none had been blessed, for there were no shouts of 'hallelujah'. Although they had not won any dividend, the bride had, but I doubt if 'hallelujah' was on her lips. A hefty female who could have been built for midwifery or prison warden, panted up the stairs and ground to a breathless halt beside the best man. Between gasps she whispered loudly. There was a pregnant hush and we all gave birth to relief when the best man hammered on the table with an immense spoon and roared, to the acclamation of the well-oiled company,

'Ladies and gentlemen, and reverend sir, I am proud to announce that the bride has a baby boy, 8lbs 2oz.'

The besotted bridegroom's father replied,

'This calls for a drink.'

That was my first wedding! But I go too fast. I must take you back to my first day as an ordained man and to my first staff meeting.

Genesis or The Beginning

My dog-collar asserted my newly acquired authority, demanded respect, held my neck rigid and obstructed my Adam's apple every time I swallowed.

The Rectory study was like the primordial sea; chaotic. About its walls were pictures and framed cartoons of cricketers. I could have been in any cricket pavilion. In a corner stood an array of bats which had not been wielded for years but a caricature above them bore the legend that a century had been scored in one innings from one of them. The scorer had been my present rector. One could well imagine that he could swipe a six hit, for he was tall, broad and, despite the weight that years had endowed, still very agile. He was down-to-earth, a hail-fellow-well-met, with a word for everyone. He radiated the joy of living and as I look back I feel that he was as near a true saint as anyone could ever have been. Known as 'Happy App' he was Canon Charles Reginald Appleton.

He and I were the complete clerical staff. The only other member of the staff, who did not attend these meetings, was Ralph Marshall the verger. He lived in Wesley Terrace and kept a watching brief on our churchmanship. It was just as well that we upheld the principles of the Reformation and were evangelical. Ralph spent most of his working hours in the Anchorage. It was not a pub but a hermit's cell 'anchored' to the church wall from where the original anchorite could survey the chancel using a squint in the stonework. At all times Ralph was a sheet-anchor to me.

'I will not ask you to conduct any services, or to preach, for a whole month,' said the rector.

'But I'm keen to get cracking. I'm full of enthusiasm.' I replied.

'Ah, that's natural, but I want the parishioners to get to know you as a person. Get out and visit them in their homes. Talk to them on the main street. Just relax. Get to know and be known.' was the rector's advice.

This was fantastic! It would give me time to prepare sermons and to tidy up the neglected Curatage cabbage patch.

The rector laid out a map of the parish boundaries.

'I'll lend you this,' he said, 'it will help you find your way about. See there? That's the cricket ground and up there is our mission church, St. Paul's at Pelton Fell. You'll be in complete charge up there.'

The rest of the meeting was heavily involved in discussion on cricket. The rector's sister brought in cups of coffee and chocolate finger biscuits, which the canon used to demonstrate the new LBW rule. I walked home treading on air. I was on a good wicket; nothing to care about for a whole month!

The phone rang. In tones of an archbishop and giving an identity I had never used before, I answered.

'This is the Curatage and the Reverend John Richardson speaking.'

The rector was silent for a moment as if he had been no-balled.

'Hope I'm not interrupting your lunch.' he replied.

'Not at all.' I lied as I munched my mince. I had a gross stipend of £250 per annum.

'Good,' he responded, 'my wife has just reminded me that I am to address the Mothers' Union at Chopwell this afternoon and there are three funerals arranged here for today. Sorry, old chap, but you'll have to take them.'

I was bowled, leg before, stumped, caught and run-out.

'Are you still there, Jack?'

'Yes, Rector.'

'The first is at two o'clock, the second at half past and the third at three thirty,' he continued. 'The first two go direct to the cemetery but the third is to church first. Johnny Dodds has all three. Hope all goes well. I'll be thinking about you' and with a hearty laugh he drew stumps. I had dreaded the day when I would have to conduct a funeral service. Freshly filled with theology from college, preaching held no terrors. I loved babies so baptisms could be eagerly anticipated and weddings seemed to offer so much initiative and occasionally an invitation. Even speaking to the youth club, the Young Mothers or the Men's Fellowship offered the opportunity to drown them in sea yarns, but it was with a real dread that I anticipated funerals. If I had known what was going to happen that day I would have run away. As it was I 'went sick' after the ordeals.

The cemetery was not far from the Curatage. The early rain had ceased and, clad in my new cassock of cardinal red, I carried my surplice and scarf over my arm and walked to the gates. My cassock was red because Chester-le-Street church had a royal foundation. King Alfred, the bungling baker, had concluded a pact with Ella the Dane, when monks from Lindisfarne arrived wearily tugging a cart which bore the mortal remains of St. Cuthbert. Alfred, who had preceded the law of the Saxons with the Ten Commandments and translated the first fifty psalms into English, told the monks to rest and gave them the site for a shrine to Cuthbert. They built the first cathedral in Northumbria and the Bishops of Chester-le-Street succeeded those of Lindisfarne and preceded those of Durham. So, clad in cardinal red, the curate awaited his first funeral.

The tall gates yawned like a black hole in space. A solitary hearse pulled up in the puddles. There were no cars or mourners. The coffin was bare. No flowers disguised the austerity of the box, for that is all it was. There were no brass handles and the name of the deceased was not engraved but roughly painted on the lid. Dressed in his 'claw-hammer' suit and carrying his top-hat the undertaker advanced towards me with an air of joy rarely seen adorning the features of a mortician. It belied his calling. He shook my hand as if he was trying to squeeze the life out of me.

'I'm Johnny Dodds. You're the new curate. I've heard all about you. The navy, yes? I was in the army in the thick of things,' said the genial director of funerals.

This monologue might have lasted until the next funeral was due had I not interrupted and asked,

'Where are the mourners?'

'Oh, there aren't any,' said Johnny, 'She's from the workhouse.'

In those days workhouses were facts.

'What about flowers?' I queried.

'She's being buried on the rates, so no flowers and no knockers on the coffin. Everything is as cheap as possible,' said Johnny who was being paid.

Tears welled up in my eyes as I tried to read the disposal certificate. It read, 'Elizabeth Goldsborough, aged 78 years of Relton House.'

At least the workhouse had a dignified nomination. To my right just inside the cemetery gates stood a greenhouse and through its glass I could see chrysanthemums.

'Hang on, Johnny; I'll be back in a minute.'

Soon I was standing between rows of magnificent show blooms.

Secateurs lay on a bench. I chose the six best plants, cut them and returned to place them reverently on Elizabeth's coffin. The joy on the undertaker's features surrendered to a look of bewildered amazement. The bedecked coffin was placed on a bier and borne to its last resting place.

The bearers disappeared but I demanded Johnny's presence as I read the complete funeral service. The drizzle joined me in my grief.

'Two things, Jack,' remarked Johnny as we left the graveside, 'First, we do not bother with the full service for paupers and secondly, those flowers were the cemetery superintendant's entries for the flower show on Saturday. He'll kill you!'

I went to the office to sign the register. The big man was most affable and introduced himself in similar style to that of Johnny Dodds.

'Ah, the new curate, I'm Mr Hindmarsh but everybody calls me Johnny.'

There were a lot of Johnnies about but addressing myself to the flower grower, I replied,

'It's nice to meet you Johnny. I hope that we will always be friends.'

'Friends; of course we will. I'm a friend to everybody. Just sign there,' he said as he opened up a tin of ten shilling notes. I took up the pen. The nib was crossed. Soon the superintendent would be very cross. Glancing up as I tried to impress my signature upon the page I said,

'I'm pleased that we'll be friends because I've just cut six of your best blooms for that coffin as there were no flowers.' But Johnny would have none of it.

'There never are with funerals from Relton,' he said, 'But none of your navy larks here. You're not catching me out on this one. You've got to get up early in the morning to pull my leg.'

'But Johnny,' I insisted, 'I have cut them. Go and see.'

'Aye, that's just what you want me to do. I wasn't born yesterday you know,' said the unbeliever as he proffered a ten shilling note. I waited until the money was safely in my hand before I tried to convince him that I was telling the truth.

'He hasn't, has he?' Johnny enquired of Johnny.

'Yes Johnny, he has,' confirmed the undertaker.

Hesitating for a moment while his brain sorted out whether or not he was being hoodwinked he rushed to the greenhouse. When he returned his face betrayed his murderous intentions. He had me in his cemetery and how he longed to keep me there permanently. Friendliness, like Elizabeth, had been buried.

Before he could explode I quietly asked,

'Have you a mother, Johnny?'

'Yes.'

'Have you any brothers or sisters?'

'No.'

'Then suppose,' I said, 'that you died before your mother and at her funeral there was no one to send a flower, wouldn't you be grateful to any clergyman who put flowers on her grave?'

'I wouldn't be there, would I? But I suppose you have a point', he said grudgingly.

He did not win the show, but may be gained another point for Heaven. He was a keen gardener and grew celery around the outside of the mortuary. I met him one day as he came from that building carrying a bucket.

'What's in there Johnny?' I asked.

'Left-overs from a post mortem,' he replied.

Well, I thought, ask a silly question and you get a silly answer, but continued.

'Be serious, man. What's it really?'

'It's blood and guts.'

It certainly looked like offal in a sea of blood.

'What are you going to do with it?' was my next query as I felt sorry that I had brought up the subject.

'Best stuff there is for tomato plants and celery,' he said almost drooling in Dracula-like fervour, 'I'm off to feed the plants in the greenhouse, but you stay your distance; the greenhouse is out of bounds to you.'

I thought of the Day of the Triffids and shuddered. A few weeks later, to show that I was now forgiven for cutting his chrysanths, he took me aside after a funeral and gave me a

9

head of celery, already wrapped.

'Good stuff, this. You'll enjoy it,' he said generously.

Upon being unwrapped in my kitchen it looked either rusty or bloodshot. My sister Betty had tea with us that day. She loves celery!

Johnny Dodds had waited with me for the second funeral. Whereas the first had no cars or mourners, this one had no hearse and only one car. A young couple stepped from the car and the driver opened the boot. From it he lightly lifted a pathetic-looking, very small, white coffin. The shock of seeing it re-opened my well of tears which had temporarily stemmed after Elizabeth's service. A little child had picked up his father's collar stud and, naturally, put it into his mouth and choked to death in a matter of moments. I sobbed unashamed as I led the short and tragic cortege up the long cemetery path. The drizzle had stopped and it seemed as if the grey sky was to be pierced by the rays of a sympathetic sun. The commital completed, the young mother and father linked my arms and all three of us silently sobbed our way towards the gates. Suddenly the mother stopped. Looking straight into my eyes she demanded,

'Why?'

It struck me like a thunderbolt.

'My husband and I longed for a child. It was late in coming', she paused through her sobs, 'when he came he brought untold joy to our lives and home. Life was so wonderfully different.'

They were regular worshippers at church.

'I'll call around this week and talk to you,' I said, for I really didn't know what to say.

'No. I want to know now,' she replied as she turned and sat firmly on a very wet, wooden bench.

For an hour we sat and looked for a purpose. If God really cared would he have allowed this to happen? God moves in a mysterious way but is that way cruel? Are people really merely the tools or the victims of blind fate. So it was until we had to ask the ultimate question.

'Who dropped the stud and failed to pick it up?'

I was at the ancient door of the church to meet the third funeral. Mourners filled the pews. Here was pathos indeed. A little boy of ten years had gone to pay sixpence into his Christmas Club at the local shop. The village was called Pity Me. A reversing bus had killed the lad who was the son of a farmer. I was given strength to conduct this service, for after the two previous funerals I felt shattered and theologically challenged. A pastoral challenge was about to be exacted. We went the short mile to the cemetery and the body was lowered to its last resting place. His mother, distraught and dishevelled, decided to join him and took a running leap into the grave. She lay still and unconscious. Above the cries of distress I heard Johnny Dodds saying to me.

'Get her out. For God's sake get her out.'

I descended into the grave. She literally was dead weight. As I lifted her head, hands stretched down to assist and she was carried away still unconscious. My new clerical robes were now the bearers of Mother Earth blending with the russet hues of autumn. How I completed the service I cannot tell but even worse was to follow. I was about to move away from the graveside when Johnny came to me with an elderly, white-haired man.

'Would you take this gentleman to the boy's father. He wishes to express his grief and sorrow. He's the driver of the bus.'

My entire faculties protested that they had reached breaking point and I was about to refuse when Johnny sought to explain.

'He was so ill after the accident that he was not allowed by his doctor to attend the inquest. Then the boy's father accused the driver of cowardice for not attending, so he has come to the funeral against medical advice. Please take him to Mr Douglas.'

Yielding, I took the old man's hand and led him towards the father.

'This gentleman wishes to express to you the depths of his sincere and heartfelt sympathy. He understands how you feel and shares the tragedy with you. He's the driver of the bus.' I hesitantly spoke.

In a twinkling of an eye the father's huge, shovel-like fist clenched ready to strike. I am no hero so it could have been reflex action that made me get between them to take the blow myself. It never landed. As the arm straightened out in murderous power his father fainted. His knees buckled into mine and we both fell down. The earth about us was the clay from the open grave. I wriggled as I tried to free my legs from the farmer's limbs making my surplice even heavier with its already thick coating of mud. Eventually we were both back on our feet, while the driver stood by. The mother had recovered and returned for a last look. The trio of us made a sorry picture as we supported each other towards the road. The father stopped.

'Vicar', he addressed me, although I was, and felt, only the curate, 'bring me the bus driver. I'm sorry for what happened.'

The old man came. Four of us held hands before the cars sped them away. I reached the Curatage. In my anguish I had committed the cardinal sin. I had forgotten to collect the fees! I couldn't care less. I lay on my bed wondering what life was all about. I felt sick.

The phone summoned me.

'Mrs Appleton here. Did the Rector tell you that you are to speak to our Mothers' Union this afternoon'!

The Doctor's Tail

Paul was born one month before my ordination and the first home he was taken to was the Curatage. We named him after the mission church at Pelton Fell and added the name of my college, Aidan.

Both his breasts began to swell and we had to call in the local doctor.

'Doctor, I'm your neighbour, the new curate.'

'Oh yes, I've seen you knocking about the place, he replied cheerfully, 'and Johnny Hindmarsh was telling me about you. Evidently you like chrysanths. You must pop over for a drink sometime. I would like you to meet my wife.
Is there anything I can do for you?'
'Yes, Doc. Our new baby seems to have infected breasts. Would you look in at the Curatage today and examine him?' I asked.
'I'll be there in a couple of minutes,' was his reply.
I hung up the phone. Paul chorussed his pain as the doorbell sounded.
Doctor McIvor stood there with the proverbial black bag.
'Come in, Doc. You've been very quick.'
'Walked straight round. Where's the bairn?' he asked.
I liked him. As he examined Paul so I examined him, for I had a strong feeling that we had previously met.
'Have we met before?' I came straight to the point.
The doctor thought for a moment.
'I shouldn't be surprised because your face seems to be familiar to me. Were you in the army?'
'No; navy,' I replied.
'Were you ever with combined operations?'
'Yes, all over the place. I did my training in Inveraray.'
'So did I,' said the doctor smiling.
Then the penny dropped. I remembered. I laughed as I said, 'The horse, Doc, the gypsies' horse.'
That was an invitation to him to sit down and the whole story was retold for Ethel's benefit. She found it amusing. Paul fell asleep.
Glenroy had carried army personnel connected with Combined Operations.
Three young army officers went for a run ashore at Inveraray. The genial atmosphere of the George encouraged their sense of adventure. Persuasive liquor dimmed their common sense. Soon they were haggling at the bar with a couple of raggle-taggle gypsies who took advantage of their inebriation and sold them a horse. They bought a pig-in-a-poke, for it was geriatric, underfed and sagging amidships. The 'water of life'

13

distorted their judgement and their vision. It must have appeared to them to be a champion hurdler because they took great pains to ensure its safe passage across the waters of the loch to *Glenroy*. They commandeered a longboat and after midnight hoisted it inboard on a sling.

Captain Paget knew a thing or two about horses as his sister was a world renowned race-horse owner. Nevertheless, he was astounded when he looked through his porthole the following morning to see what the weather was doing and found himself eyeball to eyeball with a withered old piebald. Its bloodshot eyes and yellow teeth gave him a waking nightmare. A horse on his quarter-deck!

'Quartermaster! Who owns that creature and how the hell did it get here?' demanded the supremo.

'I don't know, sir. It was here when I came on watch,' replied the Q.M.

'Get the bloody thing off my ship now,' ordered the captain.

'Yes sir,' stammered the Q.M.

Ah, but how?

No one would claim ownership, but three young, army officers, one of whom was Doctor McIvor, each looking as woe-begone as the horse and in total twenty pounds out-of-pocket, volunteered to carry out the captain's orders. The same longboat was brought alongside.

The horse had no intention of allowing itself to be hung in mid air. It had never been so well fed as it had been during the middle and morning watches. Matelots, despite their rugged and carefree reputations, are very sentimental about animals. Like a Grand National chaser it evaded all attempts to capture it, clearing all obstacles about the quarter deck in its determined circuits of the track.

'Catch the bloody thing!' yelled the frantic first lieutenant from a safe distance, but too late. It fouled the deck.

So it left the haven where it would be to return to its natural environment on terra firma. On landing, the custodians of the now exhausted nag found that the gypsies had plenty of horse-sense and had departed from the town. The doctor went into Miss McLachlan's Temperance Hotel. The United Nations were in there drinking wee drams.

'Anyone know where the gypsies have gone?' asked the doctor.

'Aren't they still up at McKenzies Land?' asked Archie the pot-boy.

'No. There's no sign of them.' wailed the doc.

Miss Mac came into the room.

'Have a drink, on the house. You look as if you need one,' she extended her hospitality to the three musketeers.

'Thanks' said their spokesman, 'Have you seen the gypsies?'

'Och aye. They've flitted,' informed Kirsty, 'but they're not gypsies. They're tinkers. Here's your drinks. Aye, and who's aad nag is that ootside ma door?'

'It's the gypsies, er, I mean the tinkers,' said the doctor, 'Well, in a way it is ours.'

'Hoo's that?' enquired Kirsty, otherwise Miss Mac.

'We bought it last night after a session in the George and now we wish to return it. Where have they flitted to?'

'Doon the lochside. Be aboot Furnace the noo. They'll bide there for a day or two.'

'We'll have another dram before we go,' said the Caledonian medic.

'It's that cuddy ootside that needs the dram. Give him a lager!' offered big-hearted Kirsty.

Twenty odd miles down the lochside the weary wanderers and exhausted horse found the tinkers languishing lazily by the roadside. They refused to refund the twenty pounds. The horse nibbled at the grass as the contenders argued their case, the outcome of which was that the soldiers had to leave the quadruped with the previous owners without remuneration.

In the goodness of their vagrant hearts, however, the tinkers conveyed the officers back to Inveraray via the George in an open truck and in driving rain.

In the Pulpit

Back to Chester-le-Street, where I was in a state of extreme nervousness. Indeed I was terrified. I was about to leave the haven of the vestry to preach my first sermon.

That wise old sage, Canon Appleton, counselled me.

'From the pulpit seek out a friendly face. Then forget all others and preach to that one person.'

I had to face another hazard. Before sermon time arrived the rector began;

'I publish the banns of marriage between, er, um, I cannot read my own writing.'

He walked across the chancel, gave me the banns book and said,

'You read them'.

His was the worst writing I can ever remember and this looked like Egyptian hieroglyphics. I tried but could not decipher it.

'I publish the banns of marriage between—could this be James—or—no; I give up.'

The rector announced,

'Would those who have put in their banns to be read today please contact me in the vestry afterwards.'

He moved from one calamity to refer to another when he continued,

'This morning's sermon will be preached by our new curate. It is his first sermon,' as if invoking tolerance or sympathy. I climbed into the pulpit. It seemed to be the summit of Sinai. Looking down upon the Children of Israel I sought a friendly face. There were about three hundred faces, many of them curious, many doubtful, some apprehensive and some dedicated to a cat-nap. Immediately below the pulpit, in the first pew, I found the old lady who was to be the recipient of my first vocal onslaught against the world, the flesh and the devil.

'I am among you as one who serves'.

This text obviously won the immediate approval of her friendly face. She nodded emphatically in agreement. As I preached she maintained her heady assertations. Her encouragement made me warm to my subject and I gave Satan 'hell. Surely, at least, salvation was hers, when I descended to my stall. An appropriate hymn would have been, 'The strife is o'er, the battle done' but it wasn't. The appointed hymn was perhaps humbling to me and an attempt by the rector to put things right with God, 'Dear Lord and Father of mankind, forgive our foolish ways. 'An adult chorister smiled at me and passed me a black mint. Back in the vestry the collection had been counted and put away, choirboys had scuttled away in search of conkers and the men to the Lambton Arms to lubricate their vocal chords for evensong.

I waited patiently for the word of judgement.

'Did you find a friendly face?' asked the rector.

'Yes, indeed I did. None could have been more uplifting.'

'Good. Who was it?'

'The old lady sitting in the first pew immediately beneath the pulpit. She agreed with everything I said.'

'How do you know that?' asked the rector smiling.

'At every point I stressed she nodded her head. She seemed to smile at me. I do hope that she will be there next Sunday.'

'Oh, she'll be there sure enough,' asserted the rector.

Then he roared with laughter.

'I'll have to tell you. That old lady is as deaf as a post. That's

17

why she sits in the front pew. She also, and I'm sorry to tell you this, has a nervous affliction which causes sharp twitching of her head and neck every few minutes.'
I loved her, nevertheless.

Sprinkled

Dr McIvor called to see me. He told me that a young gypsy girl had given birth to a baby which was unlikely to survive and he asked me to go to The Burns and baptise it. The Burns was a short terrace of houses near a stream which treacled its polluted flow towards the brimming river. As I walked there

Genesis or The Beginning

I was stopped by Black Bess's latest drone. He was on his way to ask me to arrange to have Bess's latest illegitimate child baptised. I promised to call in on my way back from The Burns.

I knocked on the gypsy's door. A most attractive, youthful-looking woman opened the door to my knock. Obviously she was a Romany. Her hair was jet black, her eyes dark and bright and her skin a pleasing tan. My collar identified me and my purpose. As she escorted me to the bedroom I asked her if she was the mother's sister. She was delighted because it turned out that she was the new grandmother. She was thirty-six and her daughter was fifteen.

The room was prepared for the baptism. The baby weighed just under three pounds. So, accordingly, a little Romany became a Christian in a room which was spotlessly clean but over-burdened with chrome vases and glass ornaments. The young grandmother closed the door behind me as I went on to Black Bess.

Bess lived, or rather squatted, in a nissen hut. It was filthy. She had given birth the day before to her eighth, illegitimate child and it was reputed that four different men had fathered the brood. I wondered if, as the bloom of youth had been coated with years of grime, she would ever marry, but looking at the weed of a man who was her present paramour, and had now stripped down to an oversized singlet, I felt that he was definitely not 'her man'. The hut had a solid fuel combustion stove which belched out eye-smarting fumes. A hurricane lamp heightened the darkness of the recesses but was sufficient to reveal Bess. She lay on a straw mattress on the deck. Her nightdress was a sack with armholes cut into it. The baby was presumably white skinned but in its short life seemed to have rubbed against its mother's greyness. A pan of water boiled on the stove and Bess instructed her man to make me a cup of coffee. Diplomatically I considered it wise to accept even though it would most likely prove to be a health hazard. Between gulps, and it wasn't too bad, we arranged the baptism. Two weeks later they all came to church, including, as Bess introduced them, the fathers of

two of her children.
'Name this child.'
'Olivier'.
I poured cold water over the baby's head. She unleashed a deluge of warmer liquid which her already sodden napkin could not contain. Slowly and sickeningly my surplice adopted the wet-look and we were both baptized!

'You should have taken your baby to the toilet before you came to church, Bess. Just look what she's done to my surplice!'
'We have no toilet, Mr Richardson, and it's too cold to take her outside.'
'Haven't you a pottie?'
'No, but give me five bob and I'll get one. Care to come for your tea!'
I went to the hut for my tea. I had denuded the Church Hall committee room of chairs and two tables and given them to Bess. I had also arranged for twenty-five pounds to be paid to her from the church funds, but she was still potless three months later.

A further two weeks later, on a Sunday afternoon, I met Bess and her tribe carrying her new baby.

'We've just had her baptised', said Bess.

I was puzzled.

'How? I baptised her a couple of Sundays ago.'

'Oh yes,' said Bess, 'But Father Johnson gives food parcels, so we went there today. Harry, show the Reverend Richardson the parcel we got from the priest. Mind you, we're still really Church'!

Adam Johnson, with true, but rather misguided, compassion had given them ample groceries and clothing. I felt that I had better warn the Methodists!

When the gypsy baby was about six weeks old, Dr McIvor called on me again.

'I've just come to tell you I was able to inform the gypsies that their baby was now out of danger. The grandmother said to me, "Oh, I knew she'd be alright from the moment that Mr Richardson christened her." I've used all my medical skill to save the child. I felt it was a definite challenge, and you go down there, splash a lot of germ-laden water over the bairn and get all the credit.'

The Lion's Share

Jimmy Walton was a wily old fox. It was no wonder that he had foxes among his collection of wild, exotic living animals.

'Ah, we're looking for a strong, young man,' said Jimmy.

I had come from the bank and was hurrying to church to conduct a funeral.

Jimmy was talking with the inspector of police when he saw me.

'The boot of my car has stuck. It does this you know. Will you use your strength to open it?'

Jimmy, although much older than me, was also much

stronger. I hesitated.

'If you can't open it, I don't see how I can.'

Jimmy insisted that he had tried.

'Inspector, what about you having a go?' I motioned, pointing to the boot.

'I've tried. It's stuck.'

I walked around the car. Nothing appeared to have jammed the boot.

'Anything special in it that can't wait until you get home?' I enquired.

'Yes. I need it out before it wilts,' said Jimmy.

'Plants?' I asked knowing of Jimmy's horticultural interests.

'Kind of a spotted variety,' he replied.

The boot had to be levered upwards from both corners. I stood centrally, extended my arms, drew a deep breath and hesitated.

'It's not locked, is it?'

'No, just stiff. Give it a good jerk.'

Again the inflated chest, the flexed muscles, the determination. It flew open easily without any impediment. Out jumped a leopard! I reached church too early for the funeral.

Genesis or The Beginning

In pastoralia lectures at college we were advised to make only one point in each sermon and if that point had not been made within ten minutes, to shut up. Well, I kept to one subject and preached on it for five minutes short of an hour. The same congregation had heard a five minute address from me only minutes beforehand. It happened this way.

The old miner had died after years of wheezing his unsuccessful war against silicosis. His 'marras' turned up in force to pay their last respects. The church had been filled with mourners and about two hundred, mostly wearing black caps, white scarfs and brown boots, accompanied us to the cemetery. I rode in the hearse between the driver and Johnny Dodds. Slowly and reverently we veered across the main road to come alongside the cemetery gates, and the vehicles, which included two buses, parked facing the oncoming traffic, as no cars or hearses were allowed to enter the gates.

'Stay there. I won't be a minute,' said Johnny.

He leapt from the hearse, and dashed into the office. Ten leaden minutes dragged by, before Johnny re-appeared. He went to the first car, ushered out the mourners, called to me 'Won't be long', and got into the car himself and drove away. Absolutely bewildered I removed myself from the hearse and was about to enter the cemetery when Johnny Hindmarsh obstructed my progress.

'Where has he gone?' I asked.

'You can't come in here. They've lost the disposal certificate and it's as much as my job is worth to let you in. Johnny has gone to find it if he can,' replied the custodian of the dead.

'He may be gone ages, Johnny. You cannot keep us here on the wrong side of the road,' I objected.

He hesitated and again refused. I threatened to break his blockade and he threatened to bring the law on my head. So two Christians communed together with increasing stubborness and determination, until the mourners settled the issue by getting out of their vehicles and lining up behind the hearse.

'If you promise not to go near the grave, you can all go into the chapel,' begrudged the kindly chrysanthemum grower.

The mourners were unaware that anything was amiss, as I slowly led them in sombre procession to the little grey chapel which was built to accommodate one hundred and was about to resemble the Black Hole of Calcutta as two hundred were packed in. To enforce my promise, Johnny locked the doors. Only two people had breathing space, myself and the man who didn't need it. Audible sobs shook the women at the front. I felt that I ought to say something. I stood up to preach.

'The Lord gave, the Lord hath taken away.'

For five minutes short of the hour the words poured forth in inspiration. I am convinced that a wiser and greater power than myself was controlling my thoughts and words. I had no difficulty in speaking for such a long time on the subject of life and death. I came to a point when I instinctively knew that after that sentence I could say no more, when the rear door was unlocked and an arm appeared above the heads of the standing mourners. The hand held the disposal certificate. Johnny Dodds had found it. The family had mistakenly thought that it was a death certificate and had sent it to an insurance office.

After the funeral was over I reckoned that Jimmy Walton owed me a 'horse's neck' so I went to his farm.

'Is Jimmy in, Mrs Walton?'

'Yes and no', she replied.

'Well, he's either one or the other. Where is he?' I asked.

'In the lion's cage. Just go in and tell him that the kettle's boiling. He's in there reading his newspaper.'

I knew where the lion's cage was. The animal was dozing on the roof of a small cabin which was its bedroom, within a larger cage. There was no sign of Jimmy. Fearful that the beast had eaten its lord and master I returned in haste to the back door.

'Mrs Walton, he's not there.'

'Oh yes he is. Just stand and shout for him.'

'Jimmy; it's the curate,' I intoned.

The lion stirred. Was Jimmy about to answer from the black depths of its cavernous stomach? The king of the jungle yawned wide but there was no sign of Jimmy. Then out he popped from the lion's rest area.

'Oh, it's you. Seen any good leopards lately? Come on in.'
He folded his newspaper and started towards the cage door.
'I would, Jimmy', I lied, 'but the kettle's boiling.'
Before I left him, having had coffee as a poor substitute for brandy and ginger, I had extracted a promise from him to come and speak about all his animals to the Men's Discussion Group.
'Right I'll do that. I'll bring Pontius Pilate with me.'
'Who the heck is Pontius Pilate?'
'A young fox I have. I call it that because I cannot trust him.'
Although Jimmy had a farm, he was a butcher. I never ate his sausages.

Eighteen months later, wearing a collar and tie, I walked past a cinema in Newcastle. A man stopped me.
'You must be the Reverend Richardson,' he said, and when I admitted my identity he went on.
'You buried my father.'
I had buried quite a lot of people by then, and was at a loss as to who the father was but was reluctant to injure the man's feelings by admitting my ignorance of lapse of memory.

The day was saved when he recalled, 'You preached for an hour'.
My embarrassment ended and the man, so gentle and sincere, said,
'Twenty years before my father's funeral, my mother was buried with as much feeling from the minister as he would show when burying a dog. I felt that if that was how the Church regarded such occasions, merely as a job and rather a tedious job at that, I wanted nothing more to do with the Church and I had never been in one until my father's funeral. You preached, and every word was meant for me. I felt new hope and new faith and since then have been regularly to my own church.'
I stung him for a cup of coffee and a sticky bun as a bonus.

25

Nay

I sat on my haunches outside her cottage. She lived directly opposite to the church gates and when the weather was kind she moved from her vigil behind the curtains to sit on a stool at her front door. She was the only woman I knew with a well-developed beard. The fungus about her chin was no mere down, but lengthy hair which had turned a venerable grey with her advancing years. She claimed grease paint had caused the hairs to grow about her face, yet on her head she had a poor harvest. Undoubtedly in her younger days she had graced the footlights. Now the show still went on.

'Did that bridegroom ever turn up?' she asked me.

'Ah, yes, but not to his wedding', I informed her.

It had been Whit Saturday and the first of nine weddings arranged for that day was due at nine thirty a.m. About fifty guests arrived mostly sitting on the 'bride's side', that is the starboard side looking aft. The bride's parents arrived but not those of the groom. Two shivering bridesmaids, pretty as a picture but not yet fully awake, received the bride as she entered the church porch.

'Hold it', said Ralph the verger, 'Where's the bridegroom?' As the groom is an essential element of such proceedings there was a delay. After a while guests for the next wedding began to arrive.

The first bride would not leave the church and sat in the back pew watching and waiting. All day long she sat there. Ralph brought her cups of tea and crisps. Her mother and father had left the church and had not returned. Her brother had taken the bridal car to the groom's house but returned saying he got no response to his knocking. So the poor girl sat through all the eight wedding services and finally went home. On the Monday, which was a Bank Holiday, the rector sent me to the groom's house to make enquiries. I knocked on the door. A postman always knocks twice. I knocked thrice without gaining any response. The next door neighbour came to her door with this advice,

'Hello Mr Richardson. Come about the wedding that never was? Upsetting, isn't it? They're in. If I was you I'd go round to the back door.'

'Thanks', I replied as I complied.

I walked past an overflowing dustbin, a small pile of coal, some empty alcohol bottles and a whippet tethered to a clothes-post. Before I could knock on the back door, it was opened.

'Oh, it's you. Mam, here's the curate.'

The daughter's strident tones brought the bridegroom's mother to the door. She appeared to have been married for so long that she no longer cared about her appearance. Her stomach bulged untamed, causing her pinafore to hang like a flap of a bell-tent. A cigarette seemed as if it had been permanently transplanted to her lower lip, for, as she spoke, it just hung immobile and smouldering.

'You'd better come in', she said, turning her back to lead me through the scullery to the living room. A second whippet had to vacate a chair in order that I could sit.

'Marilyn, make a cup of coffee; make it two'.

'No sugar in mine please,' I requested.

'If you've come about the wedding, we've no news about Wayne.'

'Why did your family not come to church?'

'It was no use. When we got up on Saturday morning we found his bed hadn't been slept in and all his clothes had gone from his wardrobe.'

'Yes, but he may have been spending the night at a friend's house, maybe to sleep off a hangover from a stag party.'

'No. There was no bachelor party. In fact I saw him taking his suitcase away on Friday morning,' said his mother.

'Then why didn't you make enquiries or at least send word to both the bride and the church?' I asked.

'No way', she emphasized, 'I wasn't keen on the marriage. She's just a tarty little hussey who isn't good enough for my Wayne. I'm sure he saw the light.'

Unenlightened as to his whereabouts I reported my mission

to the rector. On Tuesday he rang me up.

'They've had a card from him. He had joined the army: the Northumberland Fusiliers. They want us to tell the bride. Pop up and see her this morning, Jack.'

Poor, broken hearted bride. She sobbed as if her heart would break. Three months later she sobbed again, the tears almost drowning her vows as she said 'I will' to her first groom's best friend, who would have failed an army medical examination anyway.

Near to the bride's home lived Mrs Watters. I decided to call on her on my way from the jaded, jilted Jill. Mrs Watters could be referred to as 'a character'. Her displeasure was directed against anyone who tried to pronounce her surname politely to rhyme with 'daughters'. She was well educated and could hold a stimulating and challenging conversation. She was always ready to help and advise a humble curate. She made lovely muffins and perhaps it was the muffins, rather than the advice, that I sought that day. As the melting butter oozed out and ran down my chin, she nourished my heart by declaring that she wished to give me a gift.

'Well, it's not really a gift. It's a legacy. I want you to have it before I die. I want to have the joy of seeing you receive it. My family might not like it but with your naval connections I am sure that it will be truly appreciated.'

'That's very kind of you, Mrs Watters, but please do not offend or deprive your family of anything for my sake,' I remarked.

'Bring your car up tomorrow. It's too large to carry.'

Mrs Watter's home lay at the summit of a one-in-five gradient.

My wee box of a vehicle, a baby Austin, tackled the hill against opposition from a contrary wind. Mrs Watters had the thing all ready for me in her hallway. Carefully she committed 'Nelson at the mast' to my safe keeping. The picture was six feet by four and depicted a little boy in a uniform, not designed until much later in the admiral's lifetime, and worn in the last century by able seamen. The young Nelson was depicted standing beside what appeared to be a Victorian telegraph pole. I lashed it to the roof of my car and a following wind down the hill helped me to break the sound barrier. I hydroplaned home where there was a message awaiting me; 'Please ring the Rector as soon as you get back.'

The Rector boomed his friendly voice over the phone.

'When you go up to see Jill Wright call on . . .'

'I've just got back, Rector. I told her about her groom joining the army. I got the impression that it will not be long before she is marching forth in battle array to conquer someone else. What did you want me to do?'

'I thought I could have saved you a journey. Anyhow, will you call at the Grange? Their daughter is to be married on Saturday. All is arranged at church. Ralph Marshall has everything in hand. Unfortunately, I have to go to a Chapter meeting at Durham Cathedral and had intended to officiate at this wedding. Now, I'm afraid, I will have to hand it over to you. So, will you call up there and explain for me?'

I could not believe my ears. This was a society wedding.

Moss Bros. suits and toppers filled the church. Nothing less than Bentleys were parked outside, yet the bride had just said 'No'.

'Wilt thou have this man to thy lawful wedded husband?'

'No'.

It was firm and distinct. It was bravely spoken but was a new and unwanted experience for me. The Rector would be sure to regard me as a Jonah. I was still only the curate and was not sure what to do.

The groom had broken the sound barrier with his 'I WILL'. I could scarcely hear the undoubted 'No'. Knowing that if at first the hanging of a condemned man was not successful two further attempts were allowed, I applied the same principle here. A total of three times I asked the question. Each time I was met with the same determination.

'Follow me into the vestry, please. Would the congregation please be seated?'

In the vestry I sank into a chair. The bridegroom seemed as if he didn't care.

29

'Tell me about it,' I asked.

Calmly she replied, 'As you know, I was a little late coming into church. The car was late and the photographer fussy.'

'Well, that's alright', I said, 'It's the bride's prerogative to be a little late.'

'*He* obviously didn't think so. As I approached the chancel steps he turned to me and used filthy language about my tardiness. I will not marry a man who uses such language in God's House.'

I did not blame her. After sending their respective parents to escort them home, I broke the news to the congregation. I wonder what happened to the wedding presents.

Burnmoor

Rats

An angel guarded the vestry door. Its wings and right arm were so outstretched as to assume gigantic proportions that it seemed possible that the church was built around it. I wondered, at first, why a certain pew, three quarters of the way up from the chancel, was rarely occupied until one parishioner invited me to sit in it.

'Now, look at the angel's pointing finger. It singles out this pew and seems to be saying "You're next".'

Coming up astern of the choir, I passed beneath the angel and executed a 180° turn to port which brought me down the centre aisle. I could see the choir doing a slight inclined diversion at the front pew but only when I reached there did I almost fall over two huge afghan hounds which were tethered to the umbrella rail at the end of the pew. Their custodian, slight in stature, was standing half in the pew and half in the aisle. She wore a clerical collar, a long, too large overcoat, which reached to the turn-up of the trouser, and bicycle clips. Despite her three score years and ten plus, she still retained a remnant of what must have been striking beauty and, despite her rig, maintained a dignity that combined with grace. Her dogs obviously needed de-lousing. At the other end of the pew sat Joe Kyle. The next morning, Joe was painting the churchyard wall railings. This was voluntary, unpaid work which helped to fill in Joe's ample spare time as he was retired. He was short and well made and apart from the few strands of white hair which clung to the nape of his neck he was completely bald. Amazingly, he was married to his wife's sister!

31

'Joe, I'm on my way to visit Mrs Gadd to talk to her about her dogs. If she had one small dog which could lie under her pew I wouldn't mind, but two huge, restless camels, which were obviously not in the least bit interested in my sermon, is a bit too much! What can you tell me about her?'

Joe put his wire brush carefully on a headstone, pondered, and said,

'It'll take a little time to tell. Have you got the coffee pot on in the Rectory?'

Under the stimulus of a whisky-laced coffee Joe began to talk.

'When Mr Gadd was rector before you, his wife kept a menagerie of animals in the Rectory. Stray pets of various species found a refuge here.'

Then, glancing at the floor boards, he said,

'I notice you've renewed the skirting boards'.

When I had first looked at the Rectory after the Reverend Arthur Gadd's death I had noticed that the skirting boards in the drawing room were punctured by several large holes and beside each one was a saucer. Mrs Gadd had been anxious that the rats should not starve during the interregnum and had daily visited the empty Rectory to put milk and bread in each saucer! Black beetles were of plague dimensions inside the laundry and she had severely upbraided me for exterminating them,

'I fed them every night, scattering dry porridge oats on the floor!', she said rather lovingly.

Joe continued,

'The Earl, who was patron of the benefice, gave her a car. After a severe winter, during which she'd not used the car, she felt that spring was in the air and it was time to bring the vehicle out of hibernation. She lifted the bonnet to remove the old sacking, which had served as the winter insulation for the engine, and saw a nest of mice. From that moment she regarded the car as a maternity wing for mice, and never drove it again. When she left the Rectory, the car was towed away to be scrapped.'

Joe began to laugh. It may have been a second cup of Irish coffee which caused the laughter but it had certainly loosened his tongue.

'I remember Mrs Gadd had the car out one day, before the mice episode, and was driving past the cinema at Fence Houses when it began to rain. Rather than allow the car to get wet, she drove it under the canopy which was a shelter along the length of the side wall for queues awaiting admission to the cinema. It mounted the pavement and hit two slender stanchions which supported the canopy and brought the lot down.'

Then Joe, regarding that the time was better spent sitting in the Rectory drawing room in his white dungarees than painting outside, told me this story which, while I believe it to be apocryphal, does illustrate Mrs Gadd's regard for all creatures great and small.

'It was last winter,' related Joe, 'By the way another cup of that special coffee, please' he continued,

'Mrs Gadd had woken to a world of snow and ice. Warmly wrapped, she went into the garden to clear a space into which she could place bread for the birds; then she noticed what appeared to be a hedgehog frozen in the snow. She went indoors and came out with a saucer of warm milk and bread which she placed by the hedgehog. This was a daily routine until the thaw arrived. Then she went out with her saucer to find that her hedgehog was the lavatory brush!'

'Well, Joe, let's hope she isn't feeding your wire brush right now. I'm walking down to her cottage to talk to her'.

I did not get very far when the object of my thoughts hove into sight walking towards me.

'Good morning Mrs Gadd, I was just coming to visit you.'

'Where is your cassock?' she enquired.

I was puzzled.

'The late rector always wore *his* about the parish and you should do the same.'

Realising that I must take charge not only of the parish but of Mrs Gadd also, I gently but firmly resisted her command; I grew bolder as I broached the subject of her dogs. I could see that from the flat crown of the clerical hat she wore, to her bicycle clips — although she possessed no bicycle — she was not too pleased. The next Sunday I felt rather a cad when crossing the road to go to morning prayer I saw her painstakingly tethering her hounds to the churchyard gate.

Her care and concern for creatures could have cost my daughter's life. Christine was barely six months old when, one morning, Ethel, my wife, took her from her cot. Christine's face seemed to be badly scratched, so when her bedtime came that evening Ethel put little woollen mitts on the baby's hands believing that she must have scratched herself. Towards ten o'clock we heard Christine crying in a most distressing way. Dashing upstairs Ethel was horrified not only to see blood covering Christine's face, but a rat hanging from her little finger, the mitt having been gnawed through. I had followed Ethel and it was an easy job to despatch the rat as it was so bloated with blood it hung immobile. Panic stricken, we thought that Christine's eyes had been eaten out. While I phoned the doctor, Ethel bathed the blood away and to our relief, although there were serious bites about Christine's face, her eyes had not been touched. Fortunately it was a young rat and Christine suffered no further complications, but she bears the scars to this day. Mrs Gadd called to tell us that if we had fed the rats they would not have eaten our daughter!

It was the following day. The doorbell summoned me.

Standing on the doorstep was a man resplendent in a heather-coloured harris tweed suit with knee breeches. Mistaking him for one of the Earl's expected guests, I was about to direct him to the Hall when I noticed the County Council's badge on the windscreen of his car and the penny dropped.

'Ah, you must be the rat catcher.'

He assumed a most superior stance and said,

'I am the infestation officer.'

He toured the house looking for what he termed 'rat runs'. 'Do you know that rats never cross the staircase except at the top?' he asked.

I knew that they had crossed up there, for Christine's bedroom and the bathroom both necessitated it and two months earlier a rat had gnawed through the cold water pipe in the bathroom! In one bedroom the skirting board had left the wall and caused a three inch gap. The rat catcher investigated this and then declared that here was the main rat run. He had brought a large sack full of biscuit meal. His intention was to feed the rats with pure biscuit meal for four days, and on the fifth day to introduce poison.

He said,

'Rats are always suspicious at first and will nibble the perimeter for four days before they have a good feast. On the fifth day — fatal.'

So he placed the neck of the sack between the wall and the skirting board and began to tip the meal into the gap.

'It's a big one', he said as he poured the stuff.

We came downstairs to the kitchen which was below that bedroom and found a large mound of biscuit meal on the floor.

Indeed it was a large one!

Oh Hell

'The Lord called.'

This had no reference to a Messianic parousia, a second Advent, but was a down to earth notification that the earl's heir had called at the Rectory.

Nevertheless, Fred made the announcement as if he was rehearsing the day of doom. How did he expect me to respond?

'Speak, Lord, for Thy servant heareth', or

'Be sure that your sins will find you out.'

Fred was probably the roughest diamond I will ever meet. He was ageless, despite having been born eighty-five years previously. He had a Puckish sense of humour and a profound respect for others. He had been gardener and odd-job-man for my predecessor during the whole of his thirty years incumbency and, now, loyally and efficiently served me. Despite the fact that he lived in my parish, which was the only one in the diocese without a public house or inn, Fred had pure alcohol coursing through his veins. He nightly navigated his way to and from the nearest hostelry, the Dun Cow, in every kind of weather and in all kinds of postures, sometimes tottering upright, more often supported by the churchyard wall, and sometimes emulating a barrel of beer and rolling home. Strange to relate he lived with his daughter who kept the village shop and held a licence for the sale of alcohol; an off-licence. Mary kept her stock securely locked against any inroads by her father. Yet, Fred never seemed to suffer from a hang-over. Every morning he came through the back gates of the Rectory, accompanied by his two faithful companions, his little grand-daughter Susan, who returned her grandfather's absolute affection for her, and his thirty-six year old mule which had its regimental number tattooed on its gums. At Fred's command it would bare its discoloured teeth to disclose its army honours! Each day Fred would touch his cap and say,

'Good morning Ma'am.'

He then enquired after our baby Christine. He was genuinely upset when Christine was bitten by the rat, and for weeks carried out rat searching crusades.

Fred concluded his message,

'He would like you to call on him.'

The Viscount and his family won my admiration and respect which, despite later events, still lasts. I found him to be a true Christian full of genuine concern for his fellow men and helpful in so many confidential ways. He was a member of Parliament. His constituency was in the North so he managed to come home on most weekends. When at home he read the lessons in church, having obviously previously and privately — and conscientiously — read them through, so that he could clearly demonstrate the lesson within the lesson. He was kind to my family and many were the brace of pheasants and the hares delivered to the Rectory. His home farm had orders to keep us in vegetables. His wife was a generous and willing helper at church, supporting every effort personally. They longed for a son and heir, but so far had only four daughters and I wrongly associated their eldest girl, Lucinda, with the purpose of the Lord's desire to see me.

Lucinda and Beatrix were often brought by their nanny to play with my boys at the Rectory. Christine was a few months older than the latest arrival at the Hall. Lucinda and Malcolm were having a marvellous tomboy escapade in the Rectory gardens when Nanny announced it was time to go home. Lucinda protested. She found such fun playing with Malcolm and Paul that she had no wish to terminate it, no doubt also knowing that a bath awaited her at the Hall.

'I'm not going', said the little girl.

Nanny replied,

'Lucinda you must come.'

'Don't tell me what I must do', retorted the indignant juvenile, 'If you speak to me like that again I shall spit at you. In fact that's a good idea.'

In a spirit of bravado before the boys she put her idea into practical effect. I do not know what amazed me most, the amount of projected saliva or the deadly accuracy in which it sped to its objective. Nanny had no time to take evasive action and was the recipient of a goodly sized deluge. Ethel led Nanny to the bathroom while I laid Lucinda across my knee and smacked her backside.

So it was with trepidation that I approached the Hall awaiting a reprimand for my reprimand!

Claude the butler opened the door. He never addressed me as 'Rector' but invariably as 'Chaplain' but made it sound as if it naturally followed 'Charlie'.

'Good afternoon Chaplin, His Lordship is expecting you.' Claude led me into the Drawing Room.

The Lady sat there alone and upon my entry arose and welcomed me.

'Claude bring in the tea.'

They knew at the Hall, indeed the whole parish knew, that whereas Fred never drank water, I never drank tea, but Claude also had the splendid mis-apprehension that an ex-sailor needed rum, not milk, added to his coffee. His Lordship came into the room ahead of Claude and together we had a most pleasant, amicable tea in truly traditional British surroundings. The Lord looked every inch a descendent of the 'Red Boy' and we talked of ships and sealing wax in a happy relaxed manner until her Ladyship

remarked,
'I understand you whacked Lucinda yesterday.'
Phew, this is it, I thought.

She went on, 'I'm so pleased; don't hesitate to do the same at any time you feel it's necessary. She seems to have learnt her lesson and she'll come downstairs to apologise before you leave.'

Then, they came to the purpose of our meeting. They wished to have their baby baptised and wanted to fix a time, a day and a place for the christening. A month ahead on a Sunday at three o'clock. We had a long chat about it and the names of the god-parents were submitted to me. One was a Peer of the realm, another was his brother, a knight, one god-mother was a Duchess and the other the daughter of a Peer, Lady Jane. At one time or another I had met all these god-parents when they had been guests, previously, at the Hall. 'The baby's name is to be Rose Diana', said her Ladyship.

A week or so before the baptism her Ladyship fell victim to influenza. On the Sunday of the christening she was still not fully recovered and the weather was damp and cold. We decided that the service should be held in the drawing room of the hall with the receiving of the child into the church to be held at a later date.

There existed a stone, Saxon, and allegedly portable, font which lay behind the organ. I went to take it across to the Rectory to be cleaned. I found it full of sweet wrappers, cigarette packets and bat droppings. I almost slipped half a dozen discs in my back trying to lift it. The local newspaper reporter-cum-photographer had turned up at the church early. At his request I rang to obtain the family's permission for him to accompany me to the Hall. I, however, laid a condition upon him. He had to carry the font.
'No trouble at all', he said.
He tried to lift it. He was quite bow-legged under the strain, but I gave him full marks, for he managed to get it to the Rectory, clean it for me and get it into his car.

The chairs and settees were arranged in semi-circles facing the long windows in the south wall. The log fire gave a cheerful glow as the cream of British society gathered in the drawing room. The baby, wearing a christening robe that was nearly 200 years old, lay peacefully, oblivious to the import of the moment, in the arms of Lady Jane.

The service commenced on time. The god-parents pledged their vows and the big moment arrived. I approached Lady Jane who surrendered the still sleeping baby to me.
'Name this child.'
Lady Jane looked shocked. The silence lasted a century. She then gasped,
'Oh, hell'

Without batting an eyelid, I repeated after her, 'Oh hell'. I walked towards the font.
'No, no', cried Lady Jane. 'I mean, oh hell, I've forgotten!'

I whispered the name Rose Diana, but the damage was done. From that moment the girl was known in the family circle as 'Oh Hell'!

When Lucinda, now married with two sons, Huckleberry and Barnaby, called on me in later years she gave me this message.
'Oh Hell sends her love. By the way do you know of any particularly interesting lavatory seats. I'm writing a book about them!'

I did. I had once possessed a 'three-seater' and further, had used one in Toulon which had two glass eyes fixed to it!

Bebe

Every Tuesday evening during the winter months our men's discussion group met in the Rectory. We had discussed whether or not Judas Iscariot and Pontius Pilate were the innocent pawns of God's purpose and Ethel now sat with us as we drank coffee. Bruce, my dog, patronised these meetings, not merely because we had some meaty subject, but that when the coffee arrived he was well fed with biscuit morsels from the indulging males.

'Rector, what do you think of spiritualism?' came one question.

'I feel quite sure that there is something in it, but I'm not quite sure if it is a good thing with which to tamper. Is it right, I ask, to try to conjure up the spirits of the departed?'

'I know that there are many charlatans and frauds but we cannot lightly dismiss the adherence to the movement by many sincere and intelligent people.'

A small man given to reading Sherlock Holmes contributed,

'Conan-Doyle was a spiritualist. So was Sir Oliver Lodge.'

After a most interesting discussion I declared,

'Mr Wilson, who prints our church magazine, is a leading spiritualist at Chester-le-Street. I'll ask him to come along to our next meeting.'

That meeting became so involved and interesting that worried wives rang the Rectory after midnight to enquire the whereabout of their spouses. I assured them that the only women who might be employing their seductive powers upon their husbands were out of this world. By popular demand, and to allay suspicions, we broke our rules and allowed the wives to attend the second meeting at which Mr Wilson really whetted their spiritual appetites.

At that time an internationally known journalist, Hannan Swaffer, was touring the world giving lectures on spiritualism and sitting in on seances. His main assistant had, on this tour, not accompanied him but was at her home in Gateshead. Her name was Edith. I had never met her and had only heard of her in an incidental remark made by Mr Wilson. Dressed in a light grey suit and wearing a collar and tie and without telling anyone of my intention, I called upon her. Her home was pleasantly situated near Saltwell Park and I rather fancy that the house was late Georgian. She opened the door.

'Come in', she invited.

'But you don't know me', I exclaimed.

'No, but I was told only five minutes ago to expect you.'

'Who told you?' I asked with increasing interest.

'Bebe, my little spirit guide.'

The drawing room overlooked the park with its trees and flower beds. The afternoon sun streamed joyfully through the windows touching the chintz covers of the comfortable chairs. There was nothing ghostly or mysterious in the surroundings. I felt absolutely at ease with such a gracious and charming lady.

I faced her as she said,

'Don't tell me anything about yourself. Bebe will speak with you. In fact she's trying to push me aside already.'

'Well, I'll not tell you anything about me, but will you tell me about Bebe?'

'Yes. She was only twelve years of age when she and her father were drowned in the English Channel. Their little wooden ship foundered on its way to England in the eighteenth century. Her father was French and her mother English and seriously ill at their home in Canterbury. For obvious reasons Bebe does not like the sea. Before she controls me I would say two things. Her eyes are blue. Mine as you can see are, dark brown. I am told that when Bebe takes over from me that my eyes go blue and my voice is that of a little girl.'

'Well, you've given me a suggestion that your eyes go blue so I may well imagine that to be so. Auto-suggestion?' I offered.

'Use your own judgement. The second thing I wish to say is please do not keep her for more than ten minutes. A longer period could prove harmful to me. Now, clasp your hands. Ready? Do not speak until Bebe says "Hello".'

When Edith lifted her head she spoke with the voice of a young girl. I concentrated my intense scrutiny upon her eyes. I am ready to swear that a blue haze hid the dark-brown of Edith's eyes.

'Hello John'. The voice was Bebe's.

I replied 'That's a good guess for every other man in Britain is called John.'

'Yes, but not John Richardson.'

'Tell me my middle name.'

'You don't have one', said the tinkling voice.
'Then tell me what work I do.'

There was a silence for a moment, then a delightful, disarming laugh. Edith had put both her hands together in praying position and the laughter said, 'Let us pray. We have a priest.'

Still testing I asked, 'Bring my mother to me.' Again the happy laughter and the reply. 'Your mother is not yet with us. You have her for another two years.'

In fact, mother passed away two years and one month after this seance.

'Let me sing you a song', chirped Bebe.

It was a French song and was followed by an English ballad. Eventually, without any knowledge or notice of the passing of time, I said, goodbye to my new, little French acquaintance, fully believing that I had talked and listened to her, even though for two centuries she had been in the spirit. Edith was restored to her own consciousness but was thoroughly exhausted. It had been an unforgettable and convincing experience. Edith died before my mother, although I did have a second session with Bebe.

Bruce, my Scotch terrier, had been given to us as a wedding present. The morning after my first experience with Bebe my mother found him dead beneath an apple tree.

One month later a fortune teller who was due to operate at our garden party, fell downstairs and broke her hip. If she had been a genuine seer then she would never have gone upstairs. The bright yellow posters plastered about the parish indicated that a fortune teller would be in attendance at the fete. I was therefore obliged to conform to the advertising description and seek another fortune teller.

A parishioner Mrs Thornton said,
'I know of a spiritualist who lives in Hetton. She might come.'
'Good, I'll give her a ring. What's her number?'
'She's not on the phone. I'll give you her address', said the helpful old lady.

Like Edith, the spiritualist answered my knock on her door

with, 'Come in. I'm expecting you'.

I began to think that this was a stock-in-trade greeting. I had never before met this woman and I was again wearing a collar and tie.

'You cannot be expecting me. I told no one that I was coming except Mrs Thornton who could not have contacted you.'

'The spirits told me ten minutes ago.'

I entered the parlour. Obviously it was little used and smelt rather musty. The light was dim as the curtains were heavy and partly drawn. The chair was upright. I sat down.

'Before you say anything, please put your hand near to your right knee.'

I did so.

'Now, gently move it as if you were stroking the head of a dog — your dog Bruce. He died less than a month ago. He is sitting beside you. Stroke him. Speak to him. He is happy now, he is often at your knee, so please, stroke him.'

'I am a spiritualist and not a fortune teller', she said as she graciously declined my invitation to officiate at my garden party.

What did I do?

A Hindu officer, serving on board an Indian conveyor ship which was in the Tyne, sat in the Flying Angel Club at South

44

Shields having tea with me.

'My father is a Hindu priest', he told me proudly.

Having some faint idea that Palmistry is involved in the Hindu faith, I got the officer to read my palm. He ended up in a brightly decorated garden tent telling fortunes at my fete!

Bishopton

Via Lucis: Via Crucis

Adam was the first known vicar of Bishopton. He died in 1290 of old age. The next vicar was Robert de Eden who was followed by Thomas de Hoo. Following this oriental element were four Richards until eventually John VII ceased his eccumenical excursions and dropped anchor at Bishopton, after a spell at sea.

The ancient market cross had withstood the ravages of centuries of varying weather, but had crumbled, as is the fate of us all, into dust. The Reverend Charles Henry Ford, father of ten children, who insulated his study because of them, replaced the cross with an exact replica in 1883, which bore the motto of my college 'Via lucis, Via crucis'. 'The way of light is the way of the Cross'. Ford was perhaps the best remembered of the nineteenth century vicars of Bishopton. His son was at General Gordon's side when Gordon was murdered in Khartoum and he erected, upon his return home, the very first memorial to Chinese Gordon in the vicarage garden.

Bishopton lies north of the River Tees and is bounded on three sides by the Bishopton Beck. The countryside is open and pleasant with distant views of the Cleveland Hills. The church stands on high ground in the centre of the village. To the south of the church lies the Vicarage, to the west the pub and pump and to the north, Willie Twizell's Town Farm. Between them all is the village green, bearing two crosses, one a war memorial.

In 1700 the Vicar, Michael Ethelston, bought two

shepherd's cottages and converted them into a vicarage, adding an extension. Apart from converting a bedroom into a bathroom there had been no modernisation carried out until the advent of electricity. When I was incumbent, there were twenty rooms and, although only two stories high, there were at least half a dozen different floor levels. Near to the back door was an excellent example of family unity; a three-seater earth lavatory, commonly known in those parts as a 'netty'.

In contrast, segregation was the purpose for the prison cell located beneath the laundry floor. The narrow staircase and barred windows are stark reminders of this place of punishment and, I hope, correction. No doubt the main occupants were, in time past, those who had imbibed too much; vagrants, debtors and even thieves, although it is recorded that the infamous Mary Ann Cotton was held there between her many murders. It is definite that another murderess was incarcerated beneath that laundry floor. She had more than laundry in mind when she stripped her employer's bed and was in turn stripped by him. He was a farmer at Little Stainton and was having an affair with the housemaid-cum-dairy-maid, but, as is nature, he looked eventually for fresh pastures and the little lass was slighted. Truly the poet said that Hell hath no fury like a woman scorned and this discarded woman had not only fury but access to a can of rat poison. A certain rodent was the intended victim, but as he was about to eat his potent porridge his son called him to the byre because of a difficulty. The son returned to eat his father's porridge and the girl was hanged.

In the vestry were two safes. One was currently in use. The other was permanently locked, simply because there was no key to fit its lock. I had been living in the Vicarage for months before I stumbled upon a cupboard concealed in the rafters room, which our children called the 'pirate's loft'. There was no dead man's chest or hidden treasure in the cupboard but a cardboard box containing an assortment of about fifty keys. My mind has one single track during the football season, so it was late spring when the thought occurred to me that one of the discovered keys might fit the lock of the vestry safe. One did. I opened the safe hoping perhaps that there may be relics of a bygone collection of old silver or pewter, but instead there was a number of registers. They took months to read. I numbered them, the oldest being number one.

The second register was not truly a parish-record of hatches, matches and despatches, or of charities for impoverished widows or churchwarden's fiddles or pipe-dreams. It was a social history of the second half of the seventeenth century. Obviously its compiler had not been a cleric but could have been the son of a vicar or even a doctor. Its authenticity is demonstrated by the account it gives of the Black Death which killed about half of the village population. The register describes the nature of the plague and reveals the rudimentary reason for a plague-pit. The term 'germ' was unknown then, yet it was thought that water somehow gave protection, as the plague could not pass over the streams, rivers and becks. The victims were buried in a common grave on the far bank of Bishopton Beck. A rough plan was drawn in the register and the plague-pit marked on the page with a cross. Jack Kirkbride and I approached the owner of the land for permission to investigate. Jack was the schoolmaster. Frank, the farmer, told us that although the field had always been pasture and never ploughed, he had often seen human bones which had worked their way to the surface. We enlisted the aid of the Darlington Field Society and the place of the plague-pit was confirmed according to the register.

The writings went on to give cures and 'charms' for a catalogue of ailments, including charms against toothache, a cure 'for the ague' and a horrifying remedy for epilepsy which would make the sufferer desire the affliction rather than endure the nausea and demands of the 'cure'. It is also recorded that many of the villagers had a stone hung behind their doors to ward off the evil eye, or bad luck. This stone is described as having holes in it and I remembered that old Grannie Greathead had one behind her door. I went along to see it. It was a lump of lava. It was there when she went to that house as a bride and as far as she could recollect had been there in her husband's youth. The house, like others on that side of the village, dates from the seventeenth century.

As I read I came across this entry.

'Joseph Wright, of Little Stainton, hereby sells to the fairies a parcel of land . . . . which will be known as the Fairie's Field. Joseph Wright. His mark X. The Fairies, their mark, X.'

I re-read this item and pondered over it. It seemed likely to me that Fairy or Fairies was a family surname or even a miswriting of the more common name of Fairless I had to reconsider this uninformed judgement of mine when, in the records of the following few years, I read of over three dozen eye-witness accounts of the activities of fairies, which left me in no doubt that the writer had indeed referred to those delightful denizens of the glades. They were well described. Is the collective noun for Fairies a flutter or a family; never a gaggle but maybe a whispering? This fancy of fairies was described as 'little people' without any reference to wings or magic. They spun their own material, had their own coinage and ate 'a kind of whey'. They engaged in agricultural pursuits and made butter. One story tells of a farmer who repaired the small fairy plough and was rewarded by finding 'a pound of butter clagged to his gate' in the morning. It is now claimed that this is the only written eyewitness account of the little people in the whole of the United Kingdom. There is still a field at Little Stainton known as the Fairies Field.

Jack Kirkbride and I arrived at the following conclusion. Yetholm, in Northumberland, was the Royal City of the Romanies. It is a delightful, little village cradled in the Cheviots. About the time that the second register was being written at Bishopton, there had been a Romany coronation at Yetholm. People of that world-wide race came from all quarters of the globe, but especially from the Mediterranean. Pharoahs was the old name for gypsies and the true Romany is of small stature. We came to the decision that a Mediterranean tribe of gypsies, returning to their native parts, found Bishopton to be a green and pleasant place and resolved to linger there. That would account for their weaving, coinage and diet, and the name 'Fairies' from 'Pharoahs'.

That solution appeared to be reasonable until I received a letter from Mabel Kipling. I had appeared on television in a programme about fairies and Mabel, until then a stranger to me, had watched it with special and personal interest. She expressed her belief in fairies and gave me her own experiences with them.

'I am certain that I am the only one who can really understand the wonderful romance of the Vicarage garden.' After being orphaned she went to live with her uncle, the Vicar of Bishopton.

'I was almost six years old. I played around the garden. It was considered in those days vulgar to raise one's voice or to shout, so I was not allowed to play with the village children. I grew to understand nature and to be at one with rabbits and birds. Yes, and even water rats in the old cowshed. I found the fairies down the avenue of beech trees. They are wonderful trees and I understand are still standing . . . . I hope that you do not mind me writing this, but it is not just a childish fancy, because I have heard and seen the fairies in the Vicarage gardens. Mr Clark, who lost his arm during the 1914 war, will remember me.'

I strolled up to Dick Clark's house. Never dillying or dallying, Dick was deploying his wheelbarrow about his well-kept garden.

'Dick, do you remember Mabel Kipling?' I asked.

'Very well indeed. She lived at the Vicarage until she was nearly twenty with the Reverend Reilly and his wife. She was a lovely girl. Why do you ask?'

'Well, Dick, she believes in fairies. Here, read this letter.'

A very down to earth Dick took the letter in his solid hand, adjusted his specs, moved into clearer light and then read the letter.

'That's right', he simply said.

'What's right?' I asked.

'Just what I say, Vicar; I've seen them too'.

Dies at the Opening Day

I walked home, mentally taking stock of my assets; an alleged ghost in church and manor house, a poltergeist, a memorial stone to Chinese Gordon and now a colony of the Little People.

I crossed the old hump-backed bridge which spanned the beck and watched the babbling brook. Fallen blossom gently resisted their passage on the face of the water by clinging to the edge of the beck. I watched and meditated.

> Time, like an ever rolling stream
> bears all its sons away.
> They fly forgotten as a dream
> Dies at the opening day.

51

Here, at Bishopton, its sons were never forgotten. Their obscure destinies are enshrined in the registers. Time, however, seemed to have bypassed some of them. Bill lived in a pleasant house facing the bridge. Its ivy-mantled frontage bid me welcome. It, too, had its ghost; a young lady who preferred the staircase to the comfort of the sitting room or the delights of the kitchen. Bill had been bypassed by time, for he was a mere four years from a century. He smoked incessantly and should have died young. Bishopton Beck curled about his garden before plunging through the bridge. His cousin Florrie was much younger, but had doubts as to who would be the first to check in at the Pearly Gates and be issued with a harp. Bill would rather have had a pipe and a pint. Florrie had watched the burial at sea of Lady Edwina Mountbatten on her television, and instructed me to launch her, after her demise, into Bishopton Beck, so that, sailing past Bill's window she could sit up in her aquatic coffin and cock a snook at him. I well remember meeting her for the first time. She had been the prisoner of ill-health for a lengthy period and had fallen out with the previous vicar because he had failed to recognise her illness and told her that she was looking well. Duly warned, I called on her. She sat enthroned on a high backed chair in regal dignity. Her friend Mrs Stephens, a sub-post mistress, paid court to her from the other side of the fireplace. Winifred, her daughter, dutifully played Martha, and produced the best china cups and plates, the biscuits — which were only brought out for distinguished visitors and vicars — and coffee. Florrie catalogued her complaints and declared her premonition that she was on the threshold of heaven.

'Why Heaven?' I asked.

'Oh Vicar, surely it's heaven for me and not that other unmentionable place. I've suffered here on earth and I have always helped anyone, except that rascally cousin of mine in Bishopton House.'

'Well', I replied, 'I was really thinking that it would take mighty big wings to lift you off. You are built for descent.' Her lower jaw sagged. Her breath seemed to stop and her eyes went round with astonishment. She didn't know what to make of this new vicar. Mrs Stephens did, and burst out in a far from heavenly laugh. Florrie's mouth closed, then slowly her teeth reappeared as first a smile, and then a laugh, broke the tension and cemented our lasting friendship.

Bill had held the demands of time at bay, but was failing now. So, I walked from the bridge to his house. He looked extremely fragile and had taken to his single bed which had been brought down to the sitting room. I was deeply concerned at the rapidity of the deterioration in his condition. He was still conscious and able to display his impish sense of humour.

'I had better leave you my Easter offering, for I'll not be here to give it then', said Bill.

'Never bother, Bill; just remember me in your will', I said with a laugh.

Later that evening I returned to Bishopton House and sat with him, together with his son Tom and housekeeper Ethel. Slowly and serenely old Bill ploughed his last furrow upon the field of time and was borne away to greener pastures. It was two o'clock in the morning when Bill died.

Tom and I went in search of 'the board'. This was a coffin-shaped, flat board, used for laying out the dead. Mrs Ward kept the board, but she was away from home. So in that dark hour when the village slumbered, we looked around Mrs Ward's wee cottage and her outhouse and coalhouse, but without success. She lived opposite to the church. At the foot of the church tower was a small recess roughly two and a half feet square. In it was kept a scythe, rake and brush. It was shielded from the public gaze by a very narrow door, which now swung uneasily on one hinge. The long, lower hinge had rusted away and the upper hinge was secured by a long, equally rusty, nail. A catch, or sneck, in the middle of the narrow door, had ceased to function and the door was kept closed by a propped-up fencing post.

'Tom, let's take the tower door. We can always put it back before the weekend', I suggested.

So we went through the darkened churchyard, the moss-covered headstones muffling our steps, until the corner brought us to the required door. The peace of the hallowed acre was scarcely disturbed when, with one feeble protest, the door yielded to a combined and hefty wrench. Like footpads we sneaked our way between the sleeping houses, where Florrie lay in blissful ignorance of her cousin's elevation to those starry heights which she so fervently regarded as her rightful inheritance. Ethel had washed Bill and dressed him in the white nightshirt which had lain expressly for this purpose among mothballs and camphor in a drawer for many years. Reverently we placed Bill on the door and covered him with a sheet.

At six in the evening the undertaker arrived with the coffin. Tom and I were there to help. I took Bill's feet, the mortician took hold of his shoulders and together we lifted, to move Bill into the coffin. Maybe Bill had found sanctuary at the church door, for he certainly was reluctant to leave it. The door lifted with him. He was stuck somewhere. We lowered him, examined the position and tried again without success.

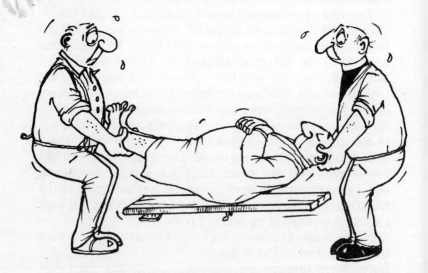

Finally the cause was revealed. The sneck of the door had become firmly embedded up Bill's posterior and rigor motis further complicated matters! The door is now back on the church tower, the hinges repaired and the sneck a silent, but to me eloquent, epitaph, to a good farmer who always closed his gates behind him!

They auctioned Bill's earthly goods one afternoon, for we brought nothing into this world and it is certain we can carry nothing out. Bill couldn't take his antique coffee grinder with him, so the auctioneer knocked it down to me for half a crown, a mere nominal sum. However, someone who was laying up for himself treasures upon this earth, stole it.

Spirited Sermons

The garden had not looked so lovely and well trimmed for a long time. The lawns had been cut and rolled, the flower beds weeded and the paths all neat, so that even the crowds who had gathered for the fête had left little mark of disturbance. So it was with pride that I invited two strangers to look around it after Evensong the following day. The elder of the ladies had been helping her daughter to move home from Northumberland to Darlington and, becoming weary of unpacking, cleaning floors and paper hanging, they both decided to have a car-ride around the surrounding and, to them, strange countryside. As they passed through Bishopton they heard the four bells calling the faithful and chastising the careless and they decided to attend the service. They had never been to Bishopton before. An hour later I shook hands with them as they were leaving, enriched by the Word and impoverished by the plate, and invited them with great pride to view the garden. They didn't know that it was really the voluntary labours of godly men of the parish that had licked the wilderness into Eden. Ethel made tea for them and they helped to demolish the mountain of Mothers' Union scones which were left over from the fête.

Then the elder lady, Mrs Wright, so sweet and lovable, astonished me by declaring
'You were not alone in the pulpit tonight'.
I joked and said, 'I wish I had known. I would have sent the sidesman up to get his collection'.
She was deadly earnest and continued,
'It was a previous vicar. I don't know how long he'd been in the spirit, but as I looked at you during your sermon, a black skull cap formed upon your head and from beneath your surplice sleeve appeared a withered right hand. He will always inspire the occupant of that pulpit. You will be helped with the preparation and delivery of all your sermons here.'
I waved her goodbye as she and her daughter drove west into the sunset, considering myself indeed fortunate to have such a bonus, and also someone to blame if my sermons were not quite up to the mark.

The following morning the good weather continued as I made my way to visit Tom Robson and his wife, Min. He was my churchwarden and Min was the organist. They had a farm which was interesting at all times, and they fed as only farmers can. Tom liked whisky in his coffee so I couldn't very well offend by refusing it in mine! Min was one who had been brought up in a gracious age and was deploring the present lack of respect shown by youngsters towards their elders.

Looking back seventy years, she said,
'When I was a girl we had to curtsy to the vicar and the boys had to doff their caps. In any case I was afraid of the vicar. He was a little man who always wore a skull cap and had a withered right arm.'
She knew nothing of my visit the night before from Mrs Wright.
'Have you a photograph of him', I asked.
'Yes. Up in the bedroom; I'll fetch it down.'
Sure enough the faded print was sufficiently clear to show the skull cap and it seemed apparent that something was wrong

with the right arm. I admit that I always felt inspired in that pulpit. Was it auto-suggestion, old Vicar Wattsford or a Higher Authority?

Gammon

There was no regal ancestor for our little pig. It was a 'wreklin', a 'runt', rejected; and was one too many for the dozen teats of her mother. Paul brought it home. It lay, a little ball of pink silk, in the palm of his hand.

'Dick Blythman told me to give you this, Dad. It's er, it's a pig.'

So this little outcast, this little flotsam upon the superfluity of nature's ordering, began life in the Vicarage, screened from the cliffs of Gadara by the solicitations of the agent of Him who made all creatures, great and small; aristocratic goats and tiny pigs. To further its hope of salvation we gave it a Biblical name, and Sarah was fed on milk and honey. She became a family pet and was not restricted to her sty, but freely roamed the garden and the village. She learnt not to root up the lawns or flowerbeds but happily ploughed the ground in the orchard. She would stand on her hind legs, place her fore-trotters on the kitchen window sill and gaze in. This amused us but sometimes caused us embarrassment if she inadvertently caught us having bacon with our eggs.

Nature demanded that she would lose her innocence, and Billy Twizell's boar, a beast of pervading odour, duly consummated the marriage. The whole village awaited the result.

It was a cold Ash Wednesday. A huge, log fire brightened the recesses of my study and cast a mellow glow over the chaos of my desk which resembled the walls of Jericho after their fall. I was always going to tidy it up 'tomorrow'. Two comfortable easy chairs stood either side of the fireplace and I dozed in one of them as the doorbell disturbed my meditations. Our visitor was from the Whitechapel Bell Foundry in London. He had come to re-hang the church bells and his work at Bishopton would extend beyond a week. We decided to give him accommodation in the Vicarage. He was pleasant and plump, spoke with an accent common to those born within the sound of Bow Bells, which must have been a requisite by the bell foundry for its employees, and had a delightful sense of humour and great patience. He was to need the last two attributes before the day was done. We nicknamed our new friend 'Harry Lime'.

'Come in. Get warmed by the fire. Have a hot drink now and after the Lenten evening service, Ethel will give us all our evening meal.'

Poor old Harry was destined never to partake of that meal. The service over, I was sitting opposite Harry at the fireside, when Ethel showed her face around the door.

'Are you alright? I'll just go and see if Sarah is OK before I serve the meal.'

As swift as a grunt from a pig, Ethel returned carrying in her hand a piglet.

'Quick', she said, 'Get a box or something. Sarah has started to farrow and is eating the little ones', and she dumped the new born member of the swine population into Harry's lap. Harry, being a Londoner, had never experienced a first hand acquaintance with any animal other than a kitten. He was non-plussed. He was gentle. He was fatherly like a benevolent hog. He snorted and puffed and his eyes were filled with concern as the wee pig endeavoured to suckle his little finger. I went in search of a carton and having found one placed it near to the fire. With caressing carefulness Harry placed the little creature in the box just as Ethel came bursting in with another. When, after two hours, six little pigs added to the occupants of the study, another box had to be found. Wee piggies are lively and despite their new born status, managed to climb out of the boxes and scamper about the room. While Harry wallowed on all fours seeking to retrieve the rebels, others got free and Harry got frustrated but accepted the challenge. It was two o'clock in the morning

before an exhausted human trio finally saw twelve little pigs snoozing in their house of cardboard. Ethel like a good midwife, remained on watch all night. Harry went to bed hungry. Anyway I didn't think he would appreciate the boiled ham. At eight weeks the pigs were sold; they went like proverbial pigs, to market. So did Ethel — to buy a washing machine with the proceeds and the first thing in it was the study carpet.

Sarah became a good mother to three more litters and again went to renew her acquaintance with her paramour. It was midsummer and the weather was hot. Billy Twizell's mother was expected to pass away that day, so when I opened the door to him and saw him with tears coursing down his suntanned cheeks, I guessed the reason. He was so upset that I felt his misery and shared his emotions, and with deep and heartfelt sympathy, invited him into the house. Like the comforters of Job we sat in silence for a while, 'For that thing which is greatly feared is come upon me, and that which I was afraid of is come unto me'. I kept silent as Billy, in abject misery, dropped his eyes from my pitying gaze and contemplated the deck. 'And none spake a word unto him; for they saw that his grief was very great'. Then, choking back his sorrow, with great courage he found his voice and said,

'I don't know how to tell you, Vicar, but Sarah is dead. I've just found her beneath an old cart.'

A postmortem examination failed to reveal whether she had died of sunstroke or of love. There was a quarry on the village outskirts which was being filled and we decided to give her a decent burial there. The kennel master came round to me saying,

'Deliver her not unto the pit, for I have found a ransom'.

For two pounds was I to play Judas to poor old Sarah? No, she deserved our last respects, and borne on Billy's trailer she went to her last resting place, full fifteen fathoms down, in a disused quarry.

Sarah's son was Isaac and 'Isaac went out to meditate in the field at eventide and he lifted up his eyes and saw . . . and Rebecca lifted up her eyes and saw Isaac'. Rebecca had come with this blessing, 'Be thou the mother of thousands of millions', so we thought that it was logical to call our next pig Rebecca and to expect a handsome return from a recurring market. 'Now Rebecca was very fair to look upon' did not apply to our acquisition. Unlike her Biblical namesake, she was rebellious, obstinate and a rutter. She ploughed up my lawns, devoured the roses and continually escaped.

The day before the garden party, Rebecca, in one short hour of unsuspected freedom, laid waste all the weeks of work in the garden. Emergency squads of willing helpers worked to repair the damage and Tom Robson vowed to frustrate the knavish tricks of the errant sow. He dug a trench one yard deep around her pig pen and buried the base of the pig wire so deep and secure that only a bulldozer would shift it. The bulldozer was Rebecca. The problem was finally solved. Fred Wright gave me the market price for her and carted her off to his farm.

When she farrowed, all her piglets were dead. They had been squashed to death when she squeezed under the wire. Then Rebecca took ill. So did Fred's old dad, Willie.

As Willie's health deteriorated and his eighty-five years were obviously not going to be extended, Fred earmarked Rebecca for the funeral tea. The whisky-saturated marrow of

Willie's bones gave him lingering strength but he battled against the inevitable, as did the pig. Fred prayed that the pig would outlive the old man so he could slaughter it before it died. If it succumbed to a natural conclusion then the law forbid its carcass to be eaten by humans. Fred's prayers were answered. Willie passed away and Fred slaughtered Rebecca.

I went up to the farm to offer my condolences and to arrange Willie's funeral. Fred was out, obtaining permission for the slaughter. Connie asked me to have 'a last look' at the deceased. Willie lay on a single bed, shrouded in a clean white sheet. His aged face had relaxed, a wisp of white hair caressed his pale brow and the wrinkles of time were all ironed out. He looked at peace.

Connie looked at the stairs.

'We'll never get a coffin up those stairs', she said.

The stairway was indeed the steepest that I have ever seen and extremely narrow and I could well imagine the difficulty of bringing the smallest of coffins up that way. I could not imagine the solution either, but Connie could.

'You carry him downstairs, Jack. I'll put him on your back.'

Willie seemed reluctant to be manipulated and Connie wrestled with his limbs, entangling them with her own like string around a brush, until finally she somehow succeeded in draping him over my shoulders. He was a dead weight. His loose arms swung crazily down my sides. Connie went on ahead of me in case I slipped, for then I would have a soft landing on an ample cushion. Slowly, I squeezed down the stairs with a clammy old Willie clinging to my back. When his dangling arms finally reached sea level in the passage, Connie pondered,

'Now where will we put him? It must be in the parlour. Hang on to him until I dismantle his bed and bring it down.'.

Now the parlour was only used for special occasions such as funerals, Christmas and a visit from the vicar, as was the 'good china' and the silver tea pot. I hung on, with Willie hanging on, until, eventually, Connie had arranged the bed. The best way to deposit him was for me to fall backwards with him under me and rise to leave him to the ministrations of

Connie's maternal attentions. He had at least completed the first leg of a downward journey. At the funeral I became a vegetarian, abstaining from black pudding and cooked ham.

Noah's Ark

Horace had dusted the pews in readiness for the Christian Sabbath. He knocked on my back door.

'Vicar, a pew has collapsed.'

'Which one?'

He replied with a certain amount of humour and satisfaction, 'The one your wife uses.'

Together we went to the church. The pew lay in splinters amid the smaller mound of woodworm dust. The nails were revealed like irregular molars, but I knew that no nine inch nail would now hold the fort, or my wife, in her devotions. That pew was beyond the healing bonds of glue, super glue, jointing or baler twine.

'Bring me a seven pound mell', I requested Horace.

He had to go to his own home to find the heavy metal hammer. To his astonishment I let him loose on the port side of the church. He wielded that flailing missile like an Arabian Dervish and under its vandalising blows the pews disintegrated. We shared the task and then demolished the deck beneath them. When we were finished Mother Earth nakedly looked up at the underside of the church roof. The resulting gash, like an open cast quarry, contrasted with the orderly rows of pews still standing on the pulpit side.

The pews were old, the panelling was rotten and the woodworms had ravished the altar. The pulpit had fallen victim of dry rot. Sunday after Sunday it had been subjected to a further blast until now it would not support the preacher.

Shock tactics are effective. The great chasm yawned at the congregation as it entered the church. The smell of damp wood rose like an unholy incense. The hole looked like an unfinished grave in preparation for an impending epidemic. The faithful huddled on the starboard side as we sang 'Will your anchor hold?'. Then my voice resounded through the darkness of the tomb.

'Next Sunday bring your own stools and chairs, because the remaining pews will have been removed. If any of you wish to buy these excellent garden seats, leave your money at the back as you go out, or chalk it up on the slate'.

So began the formidable task of replenishing the entire woodwork of the church. The job was to cost £10,000 in 1962, a mammoth task for a minute population. In absolute faith I contracted with a Sheffield firm to carry out the work. They offered me seven years credit without interest. I paid it in full within nine months.

To do this I had to con the parishioners to part with their money. We formed a Projects Committee with representatives of all ages. To gain success quickly it was necessary not to allow the people time to think but to keep them bouncing. We also had to avoid falling into the rut of repetition. Every week different efforts and functions were arranged and organised. Perhaps the best idea, and most lucrative, was that of a 'Dead and alive sale'.

Everyone was asked to give something towards a gigantic auction. 'Live' things obviously meant anything breathing, except humans, although we were so resolved on success that, had it been legal, we would have initiated a slave market. 'Dead' things did not mean only meat, poultry, sermons and sausages, but such items as rugs, furniture, cakes and even the Water of Life.

The day of the sale dawned warm and promising. God was on our side and so was the army of helpers who, by eight thirty, were erecting hurdles and pens the length of the village green, which by lunch time resembled the Wild West. Then, every beast after his kind, and every creeping thing that creepeth upon the earth after his kind, and every fowl after his kind, went into the pens that we had made for them. We had everything that Noah had, except the rain. We did not have the deluge but we did have the disaster. Harry Bell had indeed sent two lambs, male and female, but only one ewe. The animals were coaxed, cajoled or clouted into the pens and the cowhands stood back and viewed the scene with both satisfaction and amazement; almost disbelief that this assembly could be amassed. Then it happened! Harry Bell's ewe was put in the first hurdle. The lambs were put in the pen at the extreme end. They bleated plaintively for their mother, who heard them and with maternal love took the most direct route to them, crashing down the hurdles, and scattering the flocks and herds. The ewe found her lambs and the other animals found their freedom. There was chaos. Men and animals raced against each other, women panicked as a box of white mice broke open, hens flew out of reach and Mary Horner had kittens. When the great round-up was completed by late afternoon, the auctioneer, giving his services free, began his extortion. Three times the same collie was sold for eleven guineas a time. One bottle of whisky cost a thirsty alcoholic twenty-eight pounds. Everything was sold.

I bought a dozen pullets at the point of lay. They were in a makeshift coop with vertical bars. Fearing that life in a vicarage would combine penance and self-denial among their peckings, they committed suicide. At least the bird-brained fowls stuck their inquisitive heads through the bars and wrung their own necks as they retracted them. Sadly, they were too thin to eat. I persuaded Mr Manners that his daughter should complete her bridal march on a carpet which would blend with the new furnishings, and so the old thirteenth century church got a new inside, provided through the sacrifices of man and beast.

Shipbound

The harvest had been gathered in, the praises sung, apple orchards raided by choirboys and now, to the delight of young lovers, the days were growing shorter and the evenings darker.

At the outset of that winter I received a phone call from the Naval Reserve. Besides being Vicar of Bishopton and Rector of Great Stainton, Organising Secretary to the Missions to Seamen and other posts I was also Senior Chaplain Tyne Division of the R.N.R.

The base was a frigate moored in the river Tyne. It had replaced HMS *Calliope* a 3rd Class Cruiser, built as a corvette and commissioned in 1887, which had both sails and screw. She achieved renown by weathering an exceptional hurricane at Samoa in 1889. Her successor as training ship adopted her illustrious name which was later passed on to the new shore headquarters.

Following the telephone message, I reported on board on the Monday evening and went straight to the captain's cabin. He asked me to help him to investigate a strange and bizarre happening reported by Alf Crodden. It is necessary in order to appreciate the authenticity of Alf's testimony to know that he is a man of the highest integrity, a staunch and life-long abstainer from alcoholic substances and had his feet so firmly on the ground that he was not given to any fanciful flights of thought or 'otherworld' ideas. He was a ship-keeper on board *Calliope*.

One of his previous colleagues as a shipkeeper was Tubby, known as such because of his ample girth and lack of height. Tubby Ackenclose was a friend of mine and had been a guest at my brother's wedding. He, like Alf, was very matter of fact in his approach to life. He had served with the division for many years and at the outbreak of the Second World War had attained the rank of Chief Petty Officer. He served with distinction and after the war became, with Alf, a shipkeeper on the ship he loved. Alf advanced even further, becoming a Chief Yeoman of Signals and being recommended for a commission. Tubby's devotion to the ship and his duties became the ruling passion of his life. He was given annual leave, and departed by train to London to spend the leave with his married daughter. He collapsed and died on the train before it reached King's Cross. I officiated at his funeral.

Six months after Tubby's demise, Alf was on duty doing the entire weekend on board. Between three thirty and four o'clock on the Saturday morning, Alf walked the upper deck as he concluded his inspection. He was required to phone ashore to Naval Headquarters every two hours. The night was frosty and calm. Downstream, from eastward, the moon picked out the river as a silver thread. On the far bank the coal staithes were silent and deserted, the idle hoppers standing in military precision against the skyline. Shoreside, the workshops of Vickers Armstrong showed a faint light which filtered through the grime-covered, transparent patches in the roof. A gangway, hinged in the middle, was *Calliope*'s umbilical cord to the mainland. Alf took little notice of the glory of the stars in the cloudless sky or the cry of a seagull startled out of its slumbers, but hurried back to the comparative warmth and comfort of his 'caboosh' at the ship-ward end of the gangway. He filled his kettle, prepared his teapot and, in accordance with regulations, phoned Naval Headquarters to report that all was normal and correct. The time was ten minutes to four.

As he replaced the mouthpiece of the phone and began brewing his tea, he glanced at the porthole and was surprised to see a mist swirling about it. Only moments earlier on the upper deck the night had been clear and crisp. Realising, however, that mists could form suddenly at river level, he walked to the gangway and looked along it. The night was clear and he could distinctly see a group of people, of both sexes, crossing the gangway into the ship. Wondering who would be coming on board at this early hour, he waited for them. They came on board, led by Tubby. Dumfounded, Alf allowed them to pass and watched as they walked along the port passage to the drill deck. There they switched on the electric lights. Utterly bewildered, Alf left the ship and went to Vicker's workshop where he told the story to a workman who was operating a lathe. This man told me when I interviewed him, that he thought Alf must have been dreaming, until he accompanied Alf to the jetty. They could then both see the group gathered on the deck.

'Well they're there alright', said the workman, 'You'd better go and see what they're up to. You'll probably find that Tubby isn't among them.'

At the Royal Navy Headquarters the duty telephone operator received a call from Alf at a quarter past four. It was such a garbled load of indistinct words that he realised that something was amiss and so two seamen were despatched to *Calliope*.

'We found Alf terrified and incoherent and sought to reassure him', they said later.

Although the tea in the pot was still warm, they made a fresh brew.

'Drink this, Alf, then tell us what's wrong'.

Alf stared at the cup for a while, then slowly sipped. He seemed to be reluctant to talk.

'What happened Alf?'

'Give me time to think. It's all so unaccountable, almost sacred, that I need a little time.'

They were patient. Eventually with great emotion and signs of a lingering fear he managed to tell them of the strange occurrence of the night. They were impressed by his apparent sincerity and conviction that this had really happened.

'We both believe him. He'd seen something for sure. It seems to be a tall story but we're both ready to swear that we accept his version.'

I interviewed the Vickers workman who testified to having seen a group gathered on the drill deck.

Alf was instructed by the two seamen to write an account in the ship's log. In his agitation he made the entry in 'The book of electrical faults'. Both the captain and I felt that what Alf said he had seen he had truly witnessed.

Alf had returned on board from the Vicker's workshop. He told the captain and I, that now all fear and bewilderment had left him and he felt quite confident and normal. He approached the group. They were, in fact, gathered around Tubby, who was telling them the history of the ship and its predecessor. Alf listened to the short lecture. He recognised Tubby's voice. He turned to the young girl who stood beside him. She was dressed in a grey two-piece suite and had shoulder-length fair hair.

Alf said, 'That looks like Mr Ackenclose, but it can't be because he's dead.'

'We are all dead', replied the girl, 'and that *is* Mr Ackenclose. He had promised to bring us on board'.

Just then, Tubby, having concluded his historic account — maybe with a deeper insight and knowledge than us — came up to Alf and shook him by the hand, not warmly as his hand was cold, and Alf knew not what to say.

'Hello Tubby. Are you happy?' is all that he could manage. Tubby replied 'Very happy indeed, but we have to go now'. They all retraced their sepulchral steps along the passage and across the gangway to wherever St. John assures us that he saw no sea in Heaven. These Spirits had come to earth for first hand information!

The Kicking Cuddy

The records of Bishopton Church include in the list of its vicars, John Wilson, vicar from 1933 until his death in 1945. This saintly, white haired, old cleric ministered to the parish during the spiritual and material hazards of the Second World War, to which was added the mental anguish of not knowing the fate or whereabouts of his son, Leonard, Bishop of Singapore.

Leonard had a great love for his father's parish, and I like to think that during his savage imprisonment by the Japanese, who so barbarously inflicted the most inhuman torture in an effort to break his faith, and to show him to the Christian congregations of Singapore to be one who fell away in a time of persecution, that he found strength and peace in the recollection of his father's unfaltering faith and trust. He did not falter or fail but triumphed in a most unexpected way, for he prayed,

'Father forgive them for they know not what they did', as he laid his hands upon his jailors and tormentors, not in violence, but in sacrament of Confirmation.

As Bishop of Birmingham, Leonard Wilson maintained his association with Bishopton, an association which consolidated and became more personal when I was vicar there. We cemented a friendship from which I received great spiritual strength and advice. His father had constructed a new vestry, the oak woodwork blending pleasantly and harmoniously with its ancient surroundings. I decided that a plaque should be placed above the vestry door in memory of John Wilson and to indicate the debt we owed him for all his reconstruction efforts. I invited his son, now my cherished friend, to dedicate the memorial. Eagerly he accepted and we arranged a convenient date for the ceremony. A film had been made entitled 'Singapore Story' which was to have its premier showing on television. It told the story of Leonard Wilson and graphically, yet accurately, depicted the tortures he endured. The BBC asked him to appear in their Birmingham studios to be interviewed before and after the screening. The date they wanted coincided with his Bishopton arrangements. So it was that the television people came to our little parish. Aerials were placed up trees amid the foliage to camouflage them, monitor sets and controls were placed in the adjoining village hall, and amplifiers were erected outside and sets inside for the convenience of the overflow of congregation we expected, who came from all the surrounding countryside. A huge screen was hung from the chancel steps. The service, relayed nationwide, was one of the most moving and inspiring services I have ever experienced.

Bishop Wilson stayed at our Vicarage for two nights. I waved him goodbye and set about the task of restoring the church from a chaos of cables and a sea of electronic confusion. As I worked I felt pain. As I have never experienced the nagging of indigestion I wrongly attributed this discomfort to that malady, but subsequent events increased the pain until it reached an almost fatal climax. In fact, I believe that I did 'die'!

I was feeling the strain of a very busy period and was exhausted. Bishop Wilson's visit had demanded both mental and physical endeavour and came after a series of other exacting efforts within the parish. Immediately after his departure I began organizing a bazaar for the Missions to Seamen. The following Sunday I preached at Gosforth Parish Church, north of Newcastle, to a crowded evensong and afterwards addressed four hundred Air Force cadets. I drove along the dark, rain-lashed countryside towards home, thoroughly tired and with a little pain in my chest. Carefully I negotiated a decline which led to a steep incline. As my headlights were elevated I spotted a man lying in the middle of the road, just on the brow of the hill. I pulled up and hurried to him. The rain was washing blood from his head, but the rest of his body appeared to be uninjured. I thought that he was dead. Fearing that some unsuspecting motorist might come over the brow from the opposite direction, I placed my light coloured car broadside across the summit leaving my headlights on full beam, and then I ran in search of a telephone. I ran as if the very hounds of Hell were at my heels and I reckon that I did a four-minute mile. I came to an inn called the Kicking Cuddy and phoned the police. On my way back to the afflicted man I felt that suddenly a cuddy had kicked me. A severe pain seared my chest and my immediate thought was, 'That's a queer place to get a stitch'.

In the ensuing involvement with the police and ambulance men I forgot my pain. The man was dead and it was later established that in a drunken stupor had staggered in front of a moving bus. The driver had reported when he arrived back at his depot that he had hit something he thought had been a dog. The dead man had been knocked down in similar circumstances on three earlier occasions.

I climbed into my single bed later than one o'clock in the morning. At a quarter to two a severe pain literally threw me out of bed. I crawled about, beating the floor with my hands, blowing hot and cold and gasping breathlessly. Eventually I clung to my bedside until I had strength to climb back. I sat upright for a while and as the pain ceased, gently sank into a recumbent position. Immediately the sharp pain devastated me again, but only for a moment. In an instant all the pain left me. I felt beautifully at peace and everything was so calm. Then I had an experience which I can only describe as slipping off my body as I would a pair of seaboots. I sat up. My body didn't. I looked at my body and I re-entered it so the pain re-asserted itself. This time Ethel was alerted and came across to minister to me. Eventually I found sleep, and the following morning I felt quite well and pain-free apart from feeling a little fragile.

Betty Harding came across from her home to ask me to go to Hemlington Hospital in North Yorkshire as her aunt was dying and had expressed a wish to see me. As I drove my car through the Vicarage gates it seemed as if the gates, those solid wrought iron bastions, were waving in the breeze. There was no breeze, no earthquake and the gates were stationary. The illusion soon passed and Betty and I were just in time to speak with her aunt before she consummated her personal

71

history. On the return journey to Bishopton I felt unwell and asked Betty to drive the car. As we approached home I decided to ask her to drive to the doctor's house.

'How did you get here?' asked Doctor Rowbotham.

'Betty Harding drove me', I replied.

'Go home. Do not go upstairs. Have your bed brought downstairs and stay in it until I come to see you. I will bring a specialist.'

By the time I arrived at my home I was feeling extremely well and re-assured. I stood with my back to the Rayburn stove feeling the gladdening warmth of its radiant heat, and laughed away any suggestion that my bed should be brought downstairs and declaring that my indigestion was no longer troubling me.

I slept that night, upstairs, and the next morning I went to South Shields to organise the afternoon bazaar. Foolishly I assisted in the carrying and erecting of stalls and tables. I carried boxes of home produce, white elephants, cakes and books. I knocked in nails, and seven bells out of the sluggards. After a hurried lunch at the Mission I changed into a dog-collar and a natty suit and prepared for the opening ceremony. In due time the elite were arranged in order of priority upon stage. Below us a throng of people carrying baskets and bags, and hopefully bearing bulging purses, faced us to endure the boredom of opening speeches. I began light heartedly to introduce the baronet who was to officially declare the bazaar open. As I drew near to the end of my discourse, and was exhorting the assembly to 'spend-spend-spend', two ambulance men gouged a way through the unyielding mêlée, mounted the six steps to the stage and ordered me to place my body on the outstretched stretcher. The crowd thought that it was a funny act especially for their entertainment and they roared their approval. The ambulance men were serious. They carried me out, past the overburdened stalls, the curious crowd and the sweet savour of warm pastries, into the interior of their vehicle. The doctor and specialist had called at the Vicarage to examine me and were horrified to learn that I was at the South Shields Bazaar.

They ordered the ambulance to collect me and convey me straight to the infirmary. I began a long stay in the infirmary and many months away from parochial duties. In layman's terms I had punctured my heart.

I lay on my back in the infirmary for ten days, spent a further few weeks there and then went to my favourite highland place, Inveraray, to recuperate. I returned to duty in time for Christmas.

Stiff Necked

An arm had been left on Flanders Field. Dick returned home an unsung hero. They gave him a medal. He should have received another for the courage and determination he exercised to overcome his disability. His little cottage had an acre of ground spread round it. He knew nothing of hectares but every square foot of that ground was utilised. The thought and meticulous planning which were revealed in that cultivated plot, in the neatness of the immaculate outhouses and the grooming of his goat, exhibited the tidiness and order of a constantly active mind. He extended the expertise of his talents to the Vicarage gardens where he resumed his pre-war work as a gardener. Despite the demanding seasons he still found time to care for the churchyard. He was over eighty when I became vicar of the parish and every week he would walk the half mile from his cottage, down the hill, over the hump backed bridge, up through the village, with its wide greens and water pump, past the Talbot Arms and the two village crosses, to the churchyard, carrying a tin of creosote and his shears wrapped in protective sacking.

Dick was now a full ninety years and it was New Year's Eve. He had lain in bed for two days and his tidy mind had resolved to begin a New Year in Eternity. His wife, of equal antiquity, sat with me as, when the evening shadows deepened, he sank into a coma. At his bedside his wife had placed a few Christmas roses, picked that day from Dick's own garden. It was dark when his son arrived to keep his vigil. Seeing the deterioration in his father's condition, he asked me what he should do if his father died during the night. I couldn't imagine Dick dying at any time. Like a good soldier he was simply fading away.

'If anything happens, Tom, just give me a ring. I'll come straight up and do everything that is necessary.'

At the Vicarage, Ethel had prepared for the midnight invasion. The glasses sparkled on the table and the wine bottles and cake were at the ready. A cheerful log fire was reflected in the baubles on the Christmas tree and the atmosphere of Old Year's night pervaded. Our children heard what they had been told and were to hear every Old Year's night.

'Go down to the bridge and you will see a man pass by with as many noses as there are days in this year.'

Mrs Gibbon had given us a goose for our New Year's Day dinner and it, with all the vegetables and trimmings were prepared ready for the final cooking. A few visitors called. It seemed to be a family custom to relate ghost stories on this solemn eve, and the ghoulish tales brought us to cocoa and buns and time for the Watch-night Service, which was timed to finish at five past twelve. A good congregation gave thanks for past blessings, prayed for Dick, and bid the year farewell with 'Abide with me'. Tom Robson and Horace tolled the knell of a parting year, then, as the bewitching hour struck, they pealed the bells, officially making it next year. We knelt in silence offering up our personal hopes and prayers before summing them up in the words of the Lord's Prayer. A blessing was followed by 'Father, let me dedicate all this year to Thee' and the year began. In one large unit the congregation began its gyrations around the parish, by coming first to the Vicarage. Ethel could not open the door to allow anyone to cross the threshold until she was assured that Tom Robson stood ready with a lump of coal, to place his foot first in the house. Women came in last. After the cake had been devastated and the bottles rang empty, we all transported ourselves to Ray Greathead's home, then to another house, and another, until, exhausted, Ethel and I detached ourselves to finally sink into our little beds at four a.m.

A deep sleep enveloped me as the New Year hastened towards its first dawn. Before the early chinks had appeared in the blanket of night, the telephone bell rang. Its persistent summons pierced my sleeping mind, and as I stirred my inner voice said,
'That could be about Dick Clark'.
The study was a three day's camel ride from my bedroom, so I humped it speedily towards the stairs. My pyjamas slipped. So did I — right down the stairs, bumping each one as I descended! Picking myself up from the quarry tiles, which were the hallway floor, I continued my flight towards the study door. My naked big toe arrived there first, hitting the door like a battering ram. I was shaken from stem to stern. Never pausing I reached the phone and picked it up. The church clock struck six.
A voice said, 'Happy New Year, Vicar. I thought I would ring

you before I started on the cows. It's Ronnie here.'

I wished him all the best and other things, and returned to my bed. My neck ached terribly and I could not find a comfortable resting place for it. When I got up at seven o'clock, my neck had stiffened, and clicked ominously each time I tried to turn. The snow had fallen through the night and the village was quiet, with, no doubt, most of its inhabitants recumbent in either sleep or stupor, sleeping the sleep of the just and the unjust.

It was the feast of the Circumcision, and I was the only one at Holy Communion. I went to the Vicarage for a coffee, intending to see Dick later, when Tom rang me to say that his father had answered the roll-call up yonder. Because of the snow, I decided not to take my car, but to walk to Dick's cottage. Every step was a penance. The pain seared my neck and measured the way in groans. I organised Dick's funeral and returned home to a festive hoard. Candles glowed and crackers were pulled. If I had been able to get hold of Ronnie, I would have confirmed that it was Circumcision.

Bones

Freddie was as tall as his horse; fifteen hands. He had a tractor which, through its long years, had lost its identity because of the addition or replacement of so many little bits and it was so old now that spares were unobtainable. Evidence of makeshift engineering of a Heath Robinson fashion made the tractor interesting but not mobile. It rarely started up. If it wasn't muck, literally muck, in the feed pipe, then it was frozen oil. Bobby, the patient old shire, which seemed to have been born into the family, was more often in front of the plough, or the harrier or the reaper. Freddie was acknowledged by other farmers to be the best dairy farmer in the area, yet his byres were old, without modern aids or lighting. He needed no milking machines; he had been born with two — his hands, but it was time-consuming and twice-daily milking left little time for leisure.

Freddie wore his peaked cap back to front as his head rested against the rump of the cow. The milk beat a regular rhythm in the galvanized steel bucket. The rising steam from the cow's rear half helped to offset the bitterness of a frosty morning.

It is, according to the Book of Psalms, the wicked who walk on slippery places. Connie must have been angelic for she could not do so, but measured her length on the frozen snow outside the byre. The cows coughed and munched and rattled their tethering chains, so that Freddie heard nothing of the crash. An hour later he entered the spacious kitchen which was dominated by a huge oak table designed for the old-time threshing days. Connie was searching in the large dresser for a crepe bandage.

'What's up, Connie?' asked Fred.

'I fell in the yard and sprained my wrist.'

'Let's have a look,' said Freddie.

Taking her right hand into his, as he would have taken the injured front leg of a cow, he had no difficulty in recognising a fracture. Having no car, he walked the quarter of a mile to the telephone kiosk and phoned me, to request that I take Connie to the hospital which was about seven miles away. It was the third day after I had received Ronnie's New Year greeting, so when I drove over the bridge to the crossroads, I had to stop, turn my body, to which my immobile neck was attached, in every direction — like the flaming sword at the gates of Eden — in order to ascertain that there was no oncoming traffic. Unlike Freddie, Connie was tall and ample and well capable of helping my car to grip the icy roads.

I took Connie to the casualty department. All the New Year casualties flooded the place, paying for their sins of intemperance. Connie squeezed on the end of a wooden form and I made my way back to my car which was parked in the appropriate place, outside Matron Carr's office. The matron was everybody's friend. Of correct matronly proportions she exuded such benevolence and concern that one felt apologetic that one was not staying under her care. Like a mother hen she gathered them under her wings. At the sound of my car she fluttered to the window of her coop and through the frosted panes she got her beady eyes on me. Defying the cold, she came to the car.

'Hello, Jack. Happy New Year. Come in and have your glass.'

I followed her as she strutted ahead, knowing full well that in her drinking trough she had an excellent Napoleon brandy. She first of all cut a hefty chunk of fruit cake, which I think had been plucked from the wards, and as she placed the brandy before me, she asked,

'What's wrong with your neck?'

I told her about Ronnie's New Year greeting. I became her little chick. She took me under her wing, feeling and pressing about my neck.

'You must see the doctor.'

'Oh I don't have the time, Matron, I'm far too busy,' I replied.

She clucked almost in irritation and announced that I would see the doctor straight away.

'Not until this Napoleon has met its Waterloo,' I said, as I refused to hurry the nectar.

As the last drop was drained from the glass, she whipped me up to the casualty department. The queue had grown longer yet Connie was no nearer to the doctor. With monarchist authority Matron jumped the queue and burst in on the harrassed medic, who trembled at such an august visitation— the Vicar and the Matron.

'I think you've broken your neck. Go to X-ray and bring the plates back with you.'

The dignitaries of Church and State swept through the corridors to X-ray. 'Thou God seest me', but it was not God who sought to see my inside, but a Uriah Heap, who dashed to obey the voice of Matron.

'Yes, Matron. Straight away, Matron. Three bags full, Matron.'

Through the halt and the maimed we swept our way back to the doctor.

'Here it is. See there?' said the doctor. 'The bone is chipped. I'll have to put you in a plaster collar.'

'Not on your nellie, Doc. I've got my own stiff collar. I'm not having one of your concrete casts.'

'Then you'll have to come here twice a week for traction therapy.'

And that was what I elected to do.

The next day I buried Dick. They 'put him away well' with cooked ham and pease pudding and sly cake. Afterwards, while Tom and his wife began the purgatory of washing-up, Mrs Clark sat with me in the now quiet seclusion of the parlour. With intense depth, she questioned me, first about all the details of the funeral service and who had attended, and secondly I was rather at a loss to know why she wanted to hear about old Simeon in the Temple at the time of Mary's purification. 'Lord, now lettest Thou Thy servant depart in peace.' Her interest became plain when she said,

'Now that Dick is safely away, there is no need for me to carry on. I will join him tonight.'

As the shadows lengthened, there was no distress in her face, no tear to dim her eyes; only the radiant tranquility that faith and the mellowness of age can bring. She died at ten o'clock.

A week and two traction therapy sessions later, Tom arrived at the Vicarage. He carefully unwrapped a picture.

'Mother said you were to have this after she died.'

When I first visited Dick's home, this picture hung in the passage near to the front door. I looked closely at it, simply because I could not make out what it was. It was a dark rectangle which hung like a flue cover. I was trying to solve its mystery when I heard Mrs Clark say,

'I see you like my picture. It's a storm at sea.'

While I made complimentary remarks I couldn't help thinking that the storm had blotted out the seascape. Dear old Mrs Clark had remembered and, after all, it's the thought that counts.

Black Mass

Our white cockerel was master over a dozen Rhode Island Red hens. He was a magnificent bird, proud and well proportioned with an extra large comb which vibrated with demand as he woke the neighbourhood each dawn. Like all the inhabitants of our Vicarage menagerie he became tame; he would even follow me about and eat out of my hand. His crow was my command and my call, seed for his gullet.

It was a Saturday morning. The sun had aired the village street and was well over the church tower when I went to let my friends out of the hen house. Out came the hens, toppling over each other thinking that they were rather late to catch the early worm, but no cockerel pronounced his dominion over them or the chicken run. Curious, I entered the coop but Charlie the cockerel seemed to have gone absent without leave. Yet the door had still been securely fastened when I opened it and there were no holes or escape routes to allow his unauthorised freedom. It was a mystery which engaged me in a lengthy but unsuccessful search. Pondering upon this, I carried out my usual Saturday morning chores. I cleaned up the aviary which had eight budgies in it, kept clear of Christine's Welsh mountain pony's uncertain temper, fed the pig and kept a weather eye open for the tortoise. He had gone on another of his excursions. Previously he had absconded only to be found a week later two miles away. We called him Galloping Dick. So, a long, warm, interesting summer's day drew to a close and I reclined in the sublime relaxation of a Radox bath, there to think up tomorrow's sermons. The water was warm and soothing, my body as red as a lobster and my mind submerged in the sea of texts, when the worst happened. The telephone rang. I decided to ignore it but it's persistent jangling led me to abandon my moments of carefree abandon and gird me about with a towel. Dripping feet marked the way to the study from the bathroom. This bathroom was massive; quite a hike from the bath to the door, and the bath could well accommodate a horse which would have been handy at that moment. Mrs Smith was on the line. She was the caretaker at Great Stainton church, my other parish. She claimed to possess 'second sight' while some called it the 'evil eye'. She was guided by inner voices, infallible in their direction and the future seemed to have no secrets from her. She was a most diligent and conscientious worker for the church, and interesting at all times. The church lay about a quarter of a mile from the village and to reach it one had to walk the length of a large field between two hedges and then walk through the churchyard.

'Rector, is that you?'

Familiar with my voice and as a clairvoyant she should not have needed to ask. My towel slipped. Wet footprints marked the carpet as if for a slow waltz.

'Yes, Mrs Smith. What can I do for you?'

Breathlessly she continued, punctuating her dramatic message with heavy intakes of air.

'I went up to the church to clean it for tomorrow and as I went up the churchyard I was convinced that 'the other side' was giving me a warning.'

'A warning, Mrs Smith? What's happened?'

As if relishing a gradual approach to the news, she delayed it.

'I can rely on my 'voices'. They're always right.'

I knew that now she had recovered her breath and increased the volume of her fog-horn voice, I would have to be patient.

'I walked around the outside. All seemed well until I reached the wall beneath the steeple.'

There was a long pause.

'Well?'

'The window's bashed in.'

'Which window?'

'The big one behind the bellrope.'

'Oh, no. Not that window. Is it a big hole?'

'A whopper, and I looked through it. The centre aisle is deep in muck — I mean dirt. I think it's from a grave.'

'Where are you now?'

'Outside the pub.'

'Okay, stay there and I'll be up in ten minutes. Wait for me.'

Wisely, she had not attempted to go in, but had phoned me. I rang the police, dried and then climbed into my pyjamas. Throwing a coat over my nightwear, I motored swiftly to the church, arriving before the police. I waited for them before I unlocked the door. The church had been thoroughly desecrated. Soil from a new grave had been scattered down the aisle and among the pews. Curiously every prayer book had the page bearing the Nunc Dimittis torn from it. The brass cross above the Communion Table, was twisted and distorted in a grotesque shape. Black candle grease still adhered to the empty candlesticks. Feathers and blood were evident on the linen and, sadly for me, the grim remains of my white cockerel lay in silent testimony that he had been a sacrificial victim. There had been an attempt to break into the safe, probably to obtain a chalice to catch the cockerel's blood as a sacrifice to their Satanic Master.

Obviously there had been a black mass. Flossie was the only one who could give us a clue. Mrs Hill was the school mistress at the little village school which then boasted nine pupils. On the Friday of that week she had her scholars in the churchyard engaged on a history project. A good place to begin such a project, for undoubtedly there had been a pre-Conquest church on that very site, although the present church was mainly 1135. As they sought historic evidence, a car drew up on the roadside and a well dressed man made his way between the hedges to the church, where he tried to enter but found the door locked.

'Can I help you, sir?' offered Flossie, as her small band of historians made notes from tombstone inscriptions.

No reply was at first forthcoming.

'I can send one of my pupils to the caretaker for the key if you would care to see inside the church.'

Her kind offer was met with this rough, rude response,

'Go to Hell.'

Poor old Flossie, who I am sure will attain greater heights than those nether regions in the life hereafter, showed her prowess by sending one of the scholars, probably the one who could read, to take a note of the car's registration number. The man was traced by the police. He claimed to have been on his way from Glasgow to Manchester and had grown weary of driving and sought a quiet rest in the tranquility of a country churchyard. He said that the presence of children upset him and he had lost his temper. All this sounds reasonable, until one realises that Great Stainton is near to the North East Coast. The absurdity of his route was pointed out by the police but he claimed his right to choose any route he wished to take. One month later, to the very day, the church at Stamfordham, in Northumberland, suffered the same fate.

We convened an emergency meeting of the Great Stainton PCC to discuss this disgraceful act of desecration. Our meetings were always the most congenial, thanks to the hospitality of Colonel and Mrs John Irvine, who lived in the Old Rectory, and kept a splendid cellar. We all sat round the dining room table, and soon it was not only the cheerful fire that warmed us, but the glowing heat of flowing whisky and brandy. It was strange that no members of the PCC were abstainers! John was liberal with his hospitality and it had the added virtue of getting everyone to talk, even if at times they all spoke together. This night there was an air of tension. Madeleine, who had one relative who was an archdeacon and another an internationally famous conductor, Sir Adrian Boult, seated herself at the foot of the long mahogany table and announced,

'Excuse me sitting here, folk, the mare is due to foal at any moment. If I disappear don't think that I have deserted you. I'll just keep popping across to the stable to see how things are.'

She kept up a constant traffic between the room and the loose box. We agreed to launch an appeal to offset the material damage done to the church, and while they were still in an induced good mood, I began to collect donations. Suddenly it all happened. Madeleine summoned us at the double to repair to the stable where she deployed us to essential tasks.

'Quickly, everyone. It's about to happen. Follow me. I've jobs for you all.'

She told me that it was rare to see an actual birth of a foal as it happens so quickly. A dozen black masses might have been under way at the church but here was urgent business. The niceties of the Church Council vocabularies now gave place to the profanities of the stable. The mare lay on her right side facing a white-washed wall. Madeleine fastened a strip of canvas webbing around the upper back leg and instructed me to hang on for grim death.

'The foal will come so quickly we won't have time for daydreaming, so Rector hang on hard, for if she kicks with the birth pang she can brain the foal.'

She almost brained me as she gave one almighty heave, kicked with her hind leg and catapulted me over her so my balding, but ecclesiastical pate, rammed the stable wall.

'Never mind the Rector . . . look after the foal,' ordered Madeleine as my blood baptised the quadruped in a kind of black mass. The foal was dubbed Rector. I felt a bit of an ass!

The Wake

'I'm pleased you've come, Jack, Mrs McKenzie died this morning. I told her daughter that I was expecting you. You remember her?'

'I remember her well. She loved to tell me stories of her life spent at Fort William and to romanticise her flirtations of the last century. She was a delightful tease. I'm really sorry to hear that she has passed away.'

'She had moved into a 'single-end' in McKenzies Land. Her daughter is up there now. The old lady was always asking after you. I would think they might want you to conduct the funeral.'

Kirsty, who had been involved in Dr McIvor's horse episode, was the informant. Once again I was in Inveraray and had Ethel and Christine with me. Malcolm and Paul had gone further north to the Isle of Skye to have a holiday with our old friends the MacDonalds. My daughter was known at Inveraray as 'wee Kirsty' to differentiate her from Miss McLachlan, our hostess.

'Do you think that I ought to go up and see her daughter? I've only met her once previously, when she came to see her mother in the old house.'

'Aye; she's up there noo.'

'Right, Kirsty, I'll have a bath and some tea before I go up. By the way, how old was the old lady?'

'Och; nae se auld,' said ninety year old Kirsty, 'She'll hardly be eighty.

On my way to the 'single-end' a hearse passed me, leaving Inveraray. In it sat the most doleful looking individual I have ever seen. He had the right countenance for a purveyor of funerals. When I reached the home of the deceased I came to understand the gloom evident in the features of the passing undertaker.

I knocked discreetly, lifted the latch and walked in. The daughter, dressed in black, seemed to be more than ordinarily distressed. She sobbed and was, at first, incoherent. I put my arm around her.

'Have a good cry; it will do you good. I understand.'

'But you don't. Oh, dear, dear, what can I do? I wish the doctor would hurry!'

'The doctor can't do much now. I know it's hard to lose a mother.'

'But that's it. It looks as if I haven't lost her.'

'What do you mean?'

'She isn't dead!'

'Not dead! But I've just seen the undertaker leaving here.' She sobbed with increasing shudders and bewilderment.

'He came to measure her. He gave me the cremation forms and discussed the funeral. Then he went into the bedroom and was back here in a flash. He had a drink of whisky then gasped, "Has the doctor seen your mother?" I said he had and was going to send the death certificate up from Furnace by MacBraynes bus. "Well, you'd better get him back here in a hurry; your mother's breathing!" Will you have a look? I'm too scared.'

I went in. The figure was still draped in a white sheet which had been set aside for the 'laying-out', but the face was now exposed. Without any doubt the recumbent figure was breathing, spasmodically but definitely. I placed a quilt over the sheet and returned to the daughter.

'I'll stay with you until the doctor comes. You've had a shock. Come to think of it so have I. I know where your mum keeps the sherry. Let's have a glass.'

The doctor came. Mrs McKenzie lived a healthy two more years before she justified the undertaker's return. His first visit had been a dead loss.

Inconveniences

The minister was well oiled as the alcohol splashed his dog collar. He was too easy in his cups to pay much attention to what I was telling him about Mrs McKenzie. Kirsty had lavishly provided dinner for us which we had eaten while wee Kirsty had slumbered in her bed up the spiral staircase.

'Och, ye must hae whisky wi' neeps or the haggis is tasteless.' His reverence launched enthusiastically into the subject of the origin of the species.

'Haggis is akin to the duck-billed platypus. It suckles its young. Aye, and it emulates the wallaby for it carries its wee 'un in a pooch. Unlike either, it is nocturnal.'

So he went on until it was necessary for me to diplomatically change the subject, for he seemed to have ideas of the sex-life of a haggis which a minister should not have known.

'What's the time?' I asked him. He could not obtain a reading from his watch without upsetting his drinking arm, so someone else informed me that it was midnight.

'I'll just pop up and see how wee Kirsty is,' I remarked. Christine was ill; vomiting and in pain.

'Why didn't you call out or come down?' I asked.

'I didn't want to spoil your night,' she said valiantly.

The doctor arrived from Furnace before one o'clock. The ambulance began its journey at two o'clock. I sat with Christine in the ambulance, holding a dish to her lips as she was sick. Dougie McLeod was the driver. He had served with me during the war and chatted to us through the aperture behind his head as we navigated the perimeter of Lochs Fyne, Long and Lomond. Suddenly, the vehicle shuddered to a jolting stop.

'Look, Jack; try to get wee Kirsty to look also. I have never seen anything like it before!'

Christine forgot her sickness and we watched in fascination; thousands of frogs, in a seething mass, were hopping down the hillside into the water. The stream of frogs must have been at least ten yards wide and their movements kept us at a standstill for quarter of an hour.

'If I go amongst them the ambulance will slither all over the place.'

Christine slithered on to an operating table at the Vale of Leven hospital and before the sun shone on the frog-concealing waters of Lomond her appendix had been successfully removed.

Ethel and I walked along the shore of Loch Fyne to the remnants of the old naval base at Quebec. In the war I had helped to design the place and stood with very mixed feelings surveying the caravan park which, labelled Battlefield, now stood on the site. Just inside the gate stood the empty shell of what had been the wardroom and later Murdo's home. It was silent but we knew that, way up on Skye, Murdo was enduring the boisterous company of our two sons.

Murdo McDonald was my friend; he was an inspiration to me in every way. He knew his Bible backwards. He was above the pettiness and divisions of denomination. He had an affinity with God to whom he spoke every day, and a close affinity with the world of nature, rather like a Latter Day St. Francis, and he talked to the creatures as he went on his daily walk. He was about ninety when he went to hold face to face conversation with his Maker. In life he had scorned the trousers and worn the kilt. Upon early retirement he had literally thrown the clock out of the window, and lived accordingly to the need of each moment and not by the clock. He was one of the most unforgettable men that I have ever met, and he enriched my life in every way. He was a McDonald of the Isle of Skye and a direct descendent of the good protestant girl who saved the Papist Charles. Murdo told me this story. As a young man he went to his local kirk. It was of the Wee Free persuasion. The old minister had lost none of his fire, and according to him, neither had Hell. He was fierce but also long-winded. One of his members fell asleep during a sermon, whereupon the preacher picked up a huge Bible with both hands and flung it at the recumbent sinner, crying, 'If ye will not hear the Word of God, then you will feel it.'

Malcolm and Paul were staying with Murdo and Maire up the Dunvegan Road at Portree. Lissiegarry Cottage denoted a dwelling place with a walled garden. Murdo's brother, Peter, recently deceased, had served for years on the Town Council and dedicated his year in office as Provost, to the

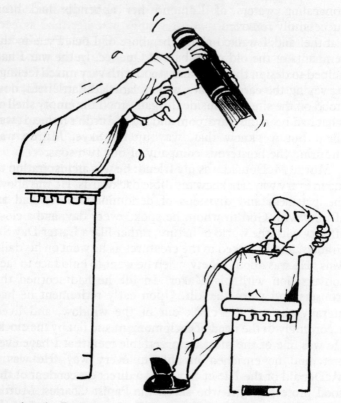

erection in Portree of public lavatories. The previous year, against fierce opposition from church authorities, ferry boats had won the right to operate from the mainland to Kylakin on Sundays. The Isle of Skye became a Mecca for tourists, but nowhere on the island was there a public toilet. Against bitter and sustained opposition Peter won the day, but had to agree to certain restrictions. The toilets were to carry no indication of what they were. They were not to look like public conveniences and above all were not to be opened upon the Sabbath Day. Eventually, Peter passed away on a Sabbath Day, no doubt restraining his bladder. Time passed until my sons were there on holiday. That week the very stronghold of Christianity had crumbled, the precepts of psalm and proverb perverted, for the Town Council, no doubt tormented by the spiritual proddings of Peter, had agreed that the toilets should open on Sundays. On the first Sunday of this shattering spiritual deviation, Malcolm and Paul walked almost two miles to the nearest church which was the Wee Free Kirk. For one hour and ten minutes they listened to the minister as he invoked the fury of Heaven upon those who dare to take advantage of the Devil's newest snare, the toilets. They would relieve themselves only to suffer eternal damnation and erasure from the Church Roll. So fiercely was this sermon delivered that Malcolm, who was not even a member of that denomination, longed to spend a penny, but the fear of Hell had been so impressed upon his mind that he and Paul did a four minute mile back to Lissiegarry.

New Fields

The Reverend Isaac Nelson, uncle of the illustrious Horatio, staggered an indirect course from the local hostelry towards the vicarage he had built at Mitford. His architectural plans had failed to place the vicarage on the side of the river nearest to the place of refreshment. So he had a problem. To lessen the inconvenience the river caused, stepping stones pace out across the intervening water but they had been there so long that, unlike the rolling stones, they had gathered moss. The inebriated ecclesiastic could not walk on slippery places and was scuttled midstream. They found him the next morning with a smile that rigor-mortis had fixed and the benefice was declared vacant. Oh, death, where is thy sting?

I had done my homework in respect of this Northumbrian parish for the living had been offered to me. Its history was perhaps shorter than that of Great Stainton and probably about eighty years in advance of Bishopton. The list of previous incumbents was impressive even though, upon my research, there were some who were not so impressive. Roger Venus had been deprived of the benefice because during his eight years of incumbency he was in Mitford less than six months. His successor, William Harte, was not much of an improvement. He neglected both his duties and studies so seriously that he was made to sit a test. He had to recount the gospel of Saint Matthew in good English by either reading it or writing it. He failed!

Roderick Charles Macleod of Dunvegan Castle on the Isle of Skye was of a good presbyterian family, a stalwart of the thirty nine articles of religion and the *Book of Common Prayer*. A pioneer of photography, and a composer of music, he spanned the nineteenth and twentieth centuries serving diligently and generously as a shepherd to his flock. It humbled me yet gave me great satisfaction that when I retired I was referred to as a second Canon Macleod.

I walked across the field at Bishopton towards my churchwarden Tom Robson. Each step I took was heavy with foreboding and anxiety.

'Tom.'

'Hello, Vicar. Lovely day, but the frost still bites.'

'Yes, Tom.'

'We'll go to the house and get Min to put the kettle on.'

'Just a moment. There's something I must tell you.'

The rooks cawed overhead as they busied themselves carrying twigs for their nests. An easterly breeze nibbled at our ears but the ground was beginning to yield after the grip of winter. I continued,

'I've been offered another living.'

Without hesitation Tom replied,

'But you are not going to accept it.'

'Well, I've promised to look at it.'

We went indoors.

'I do not particularly wish to leave Bishopton. My family and I are so happy here. It's a wonderful parish. The people have responded to me well. Church life is healthy and we love it here.'

'Then why go?'

'The Missions to Seamen think that I would be invaluable to them for their Northern area if I had a living in the middle of the region. The Bishop concurs.'

They looked genuinely distressed. An awkward silence followed.

'Tom, I'll probably turn it down.'

I did refuse the offer but the pressure was stepped up. Almost daily, Billy Leech rang me up urging me to go. The Bishop of Newcastle wrote to me and the Seamen's Mission pleaded with me. Eventually, with great misgivings, I accepted.

Mitford

Mitford looked a peaceful place. As I read through its records its history of turbulence, both secular and temporal, became as evident as its ruined castle. At times even the church and churchyard had echoed to the sounds of battle so familiar to the ramparts of the castle.

'Gawen Lawson bade the curate of Mydeforthe to com downe and leave his pratlynge, and with a lewd fellow, George Walby, did sckife, laughe and gest at the pepul who were evill trobled with a hoost.' (an irritating cough).

Later the vicar had to separate John Doffenby and Roger Fenwick during a brawl in the church which began with a struggle over the occupancy of a pew. Doffenby called Fenwick a 'theffe' and the vicar a 'meddler'. Sticks and staves were used in aggression and later Doffenby was accused 'that he did quarell, chide and brall in Mydeforthe Churchyard and did use and weeld a grevus weapon, namely a lance-staffe'.

I was inducted there in 1966, and in the same year I was laid into by a ruffian within the churchyard, the weapon being a pair of thumping fists empowered by a British, rugby-built stature. The man was engaged in an illegal use of the churchyard, in short, carrying out an act of desecration.

Says Alice

In bygone days three things mattered in the little villages which were the backbone of our nation. They were the three P's; the parson, the pub and the pump.

At Mitford the pump had not long been superceded, to be replaced by a new centre of the goodwives' gossip, the Post Office. Here one could buy almost everything from red-backed notebooks to sliced bread, but would experience difficulty in obtaining any stamp that was not the normal rate of postage. Here one could find solace and assurance, both spiritual and monetary. Here was Alice whose benign smile masked a deep insight into the affairs of man and an accurate assessment of one's credit worthiness. From the cradle to the grave the village post office served the villagers, dished out family allowances to the fruitful and pensions to the senior citizens. Alice, no longer a chicken, had a younger bird to assist in the shop. Alma attracted the teenage droolers and boosted the sales of sweets and ices.

Alma was entitled to her annual leave for holiday. Alice had to find a temporary replacement. Since the days of the Chartists the Shopkeepers' Act has laid down a minimum age for shop-workers but has never stipulated a maximum age, much to Alice's relief as four score years were surely looming. The advantage of the Act was that Alice had unrestricted recruitment among the senior citizens or more mature members of the village and eventually philanthropists were Shanghaied and the Great Hazard began.

Teenagers drooling over Alma, and sucking black bullets, were replaced by men of increasing girth and blood pressure who supported their 'leek-trench' backs against the potato rack. Agnes and Violet, dressed and washed to impress, busily buzzed about the back counter beat. One afternoon I edged my way into the shop between the waiting throng of geriatrics. I managed to find a stand against the frozen food fridge and stood, with cold detachment, surveying the chaos. I waited through demands for dog food, cornflakes, washing powders and the *Sporting Times*. After reciting the Litany five times, rehearsing the 119th psalm and singing 'Christian seek not yet repose' it came to my turn to be served.

Teasingly I requested from Agnes,
'Five barley loaves and two small fishes please.'
I got the answer I deserved.

'Certainly, Vicar, do you want them cut, uncut, fresh or frozen.'

Alice came in at this point and saw the fur hat I was wearing. Alice's lanquid eyes of placid pools roused into a flood of dancing delight, and with her international knowledge declared to all and sundry,

'Look, a flipping Russian.'

I then hastened to my purpose. 'Agnes, give me two fourpenny stamps, please.'

'Oh, the other counter, Vicar.'

I moved the requisite yard and waited until an old pensioner bought her cornplasters and another a bag of bran for his rabbits. Then Agnes transported herself and assumed the dignity and office of a postmistress. As if she had never seen me before she asked,

'Yes?'

'Two fourpenny stamps, please.'

'Sorry, but we can't serve stamps after five-thirty, can we Alice?'

'But Alice,' I appealed, 'This is for the church.'

Laying up treasures in heaven Alice abrogated the law of the land and I duly received my stamps.

Alice did not have long to confirm the treasure she had amassed by her patience and service. She came to church on the Sunday evening. Sitting in her usual at-the-back pew, out of draughts and difficult for the collection bag to reach, she told me of the pains in her legs.

'They'll kill me, Vicar.'

'Well, Alice,' I joked, 'Don't be too long in pegging out. The winter will soon make it hard to dig.'

She laughed, and was found dead in her bed the following morning. Her legs had killed her.

Heads

My old shipmate found me in the churchyard. The flowers

on Alice's grave were still fresh and I pondered on how the whole community would miss her.

Above me the rooks topped the steeple, the sun topped the sky and the russet hues of autumn were beginning to cloak nature with its combat jacket. The grass had been cut, probably for the last time before winter and the scent of its unraked relics was pleasing to my senses. I felt at peace. Commander Walker, a town dweller, also found the peace infectious.

He parked his car in the church gateway. I watched him get out, stretch his legs, turn towards the sunlit castle and breathe deep. He had not yet seen me. He strolled across the road, leaned leisurely upon the field-fence and pensively surveyed the ruins. Soon the curl of smoke from his pipe showed his contentment. God was in His Heaven and all was well. Jim's cares and frictions evaporated in the sweet contentment of his pipe while the non-smoking bovines lay in the field enjoying a second chewing of their previous cropping. He turned and saw me. He walked to Alice's grave, indicating with the stem of his pipe which was more articulate than he, and asked,

'A new one?'

I told him of Alice.

'Jack,' he said, 'You're lucky to be here. It's such a peaceful spot.'

As he spoke a police car tore dangerously over the bridge, skidded around the sharp bend and screeched to a halt behind the commander's car. Two uniformed policemen and one plain clothes investigator were about to plunge through the Vicarage gateway when they saw me and accordingly adjusted their direction. Soon Alice had the Church, Navy and Law all represented at her resting place. It must have grieved her that she had nothing to sell us.

'What cheer?' I said, 'Someone pinched the crown jewels?'

'No, Vicar,' said the sergeant, 'We've had a phone call informing us that an explosive device has been placed in or about your church. We must conduct a thorough search.'

The only explosive device that I could remember in that

church was a stink bomb which exploded in the choir stalls and filled the air with a satanic incense. The sergeant accompanied me as I emptied cupboards, threw out cassocks, collars, cribs and candles. Hassocks were hurled about, altar covers disarrayed and pews perused both over and under. The belfrey door was cautiously opened and the spiral staircase echoed to the pounding of police boots. Bellropes and bells were thoroughly examined. Meanwhile, other officers hurdled the headstones, lifted wreaths from Alice's grave and tore ivy from the churchyard wall. Nothing was found.

'Keep your eyes open for a few days, Vicar, and report any suspicious parcel or packet no matter what size. We'll be back soon.'

They left and I noticed that the peace-pursuing Commander had also departed. A policeman came back with a metal detector. They did not find a bomb.

Two months later the leaves had left the trees, the air was keen and the days were short. The winter's sun promised a frosty night but made the day both pleasant and bracing. Dead leaves encroaching into the churchyard were disturbed by the commander's car as once more he sought to smoke his pipe of peace at Mitford. Over a cup of coffee, and as the log spluttered on the hearth, he asked me if we ever found the obnoxious bomb. The phone summoned me. The central heating had failed and the hallway was cold and draughty, but the voice over the phone was warm with excitement.

'Vicar,' came the cultured tones of Pat Sanderson, 'I've just dug up a human head in the garden. What should I do?'

'I'll be over straight away,' I replied.

The Manor House lay on the opposite side of the church from the Vicarage. Two heads are better than one, so I called to the commander 'Jim, gulp your coffee and come with me.' We hurried through the churchyard towards the wicket gate that opened to the Manor House. I expected to see a hoary, hairy head, gruesome in its own gore, with startling eyes and gaping mouth, but staring at me from sightless sockets was the hideous grin of a begrimed skull. A spade in a rosebed had

resurrected it to light once more, but its charcoal frame was more suited to the clay than to the alien light.
Pat said, 'What shall we do?'
The commander, being used to Queen's Regulations and Admiralty Instructions played it by the book,
'Call the police.'
Pat replied, 'Make the call from the Manor House. We'll have a drink while we wait.'

Iris poured the rum ration. The police instructed us to touch nothing and wait for their arrival. Glass in hand, with moistened lips, I watched for the police from the mullioned window, when, to my horror, I saw my dog investigating the possibility of a gratuitous meal. Dog and skull were separated and Roger compensated with a dish of Manor House cat food.

The police arrived and concluded that as it was obviously a very old skull, it was the concern of the coroner's office.
'Leave it there until you hear from us.'

In fact it was not the police who rang us but the coroner's officer. He instructed us to place the skull in the church safe.

'But it's filthy; it's full of soil,' I protested.

'For goodness sake don't clean it. I want it as it is. I'll collect it in a couple of days.'

So I emptied the safe of registers and chalices and deposited the grim relic in the sepulchral darkness. Commander Jim and I returned to the Vicarage.

Once again his pipe was lit and the peace that seemed to be elusive, or at best transient, descended upon us as the shadows lengthened and the air grew crisp for the night.

'I better go before it gets too dark,' said the sailor.

We walked towards his car as Alan Hamilton came hurrying towards us.

'I say, Jack, I've just found a skeleton on the river bank.'

There is an old proverb which asserts that it never rains but it pours, but two lots of bones may be a dog's dream but were a nightmare to me. The grass was turning white as we crunched it beneath our hurrying feet set in the direction of the river. As we walked I made a mental note that there was no room in the church safe for a skeleton. The commander must have thought that he had arrived at a charnal pit. Sure enough a complete skeleton reposed in the hardening clay of the bank. It was very small. I rang the coroner's office again. The officer became agnostic and lost his sense of humour, and promised to come the next day, making no reference to the church safe. Jim Walker went home counting his bones.

The coroner's officer took away the skull in his own car, threatening me that if it was not claimed within six months it would become my property. Forensic experts declared it to be the skull of a female, probably aged between thirty-five and forty at death and having died over two hundred years ago. An inquest was held and I was instructed to re-inter it in consecrated ground. I never saw the skeleton again. The police covered it with earth to resume its sleep by the pale waters.

Stoney Ground

The main road in ancient times searched a southern way across the Cheviots and reached out across the wildness and beauty of Northumberland — o'er moor and fen; o'er cragg and torrent till it met the confluence of the rivers Font and Wansbeck. Here the road splashed a stone-stretched way across the many fords, High Ford, Low Ford, Church Ford and Mid Ford. Halig Rith was the Saxon name of the church ford and the tiny Saxon settlement became known as Mydforthe. Time, and the Normans, passed over the road until the sharper tongue called the place Mitford. I like to think that I, in a very real way, succeeded that venerable saint of Lindisfarne, Aidan; for he, it is recorded, baptized often in the living waters of the smaller of the rivers at Mitford hence its name The Font. I was conscious that I probably had the only British parish with a running font! It emptied its waters into the deeper and stronger currents of the Wansbeck river, the name denoting, some said, 'pale waters' while others hold that it bespeaks of the multitudinous population of moles about its banks, the Saxon name, which is often used today, for moles being 'want'.

Moles regularly erupted my lawn and I found it more profitable to sell the molehills as excellent soil for greenhouses than to remove the moles. I announced in church that molehills were for sale.

101

'Bring your own bags. Tenpence a mole hill from the garden but twenty pence if taken from the consecrated soil of the churchyard, which, after all will assure the success of your leek trenches.'

The moles could not produce enough, but they helped to put the new roof on the church. The whole of nature seemed to find its environment around the Vicarage. I could almost set my watch by the lazy flight of the heron, as it daily trailed its long legs behind its skinny body in a short cut across the horseshoe bend in the river just before noon. Its murky grey contrasted with the brilliant plumage of the shorter legged woodpecker which would abandon its bark for the kitchen scraps. The red squirrel often sat in prayer in the thick, warm foliage of the copper beech, and across the Castle Field among the trees on the rising ground, the fox had its earth and the badgers their sett. The dignified deer often favoured me with a fleeting glimpse as did the kingfisher as it passed by in a blue flash. The dragonfly hovered and gleamed in the sunshine of a summer's day. Here was nature in all her glory and often in capricious mood delighting to surprise with the unusual.

Walking close to the river I came across a duck's nest. The duck quacked its alarm and fled clumsily away at my approach. I took the opportunity to inspect the nest and saw five eggs nestled there. Nothing out of the usual, except that the nest was up a tree! I kept the location secret as I consulted George Brown. He knew every twist of that river, every mood of the seasons and the quirks of nature but had never heard of a duck's nest being up a tree. Finally I asked the Hancock Natural History Museum to enlighten me. They agreed that it was extremely rare for British ducks to build up trees, but said that Dutch ducks, because of the regular flooding, often did so. So, I informed my parishioners that we either had a Dutch duck or we should urgently set about building an ark.

Of course we had the village poet, who, on seeing me labour in my garden said,
'Ah, Vicar, giving God a hand' and then proceeding to teach his grandmother how to suck eggs he went on:

'There is no belief
Who plants a seed beneath the sod
And waits to see it push away the clod;
He trusts in God.'

God had been the custodian of a little rough plot just outside the Vicarage wall and had made little impression. Maybe He liked it in its stoney, uneven and untidy state. It may have resembled Sinai, but, like Moses, I took the law into my own hands and began to bring order out of chaos. I went forth to sow. A heavenly dart jerked me to remembrance that somewhere I had read that some other sower had cast some of his seed among stones and some among thistles. That, I was determined, would not happen to me. The land to be sown was indeed stoney, for boulders had lain there ever since they had slung them from slings to defend the castle walls. There were heavy stones that defied any bending back to straighten; round stones that gather no moss; sticks and stones that break my bones, gallstones; millstones; corner stones; hundred weight of stones, all, except the rolling stones, piled high in mocking confusion, challenging eviction. The Oxford Dictionary defined a stone as:
'a piece of rock of any shape, usually detached from the earth's crust and of no greater size than might be used in building or road making or as a missile.'
I found these to be unattachable from the earth's crust, rejected by builders and useless to roadmakers and too large to use as missiles. Thistles are defined in the same tome as 'eaten by donkeys and rabbits and the emblem of the Scots.' I had no donkey, nor yet a rabbit but my Scots motto reads 'hold fast'. I set about to remove all hindrances, annoyances and other obstructions that would hamper my sowing. Barrow load after barrow load lengthened and bent my back, slipped my disc and tore my hands. Days came and went; so did the stones. Hot baths not only eased my aching back but also weakened it. Determination to succeed became an obsession, but it conquered and the evening came when the soil was last denuded of its contours. Spadework commenced but was soon abandoned as it seemed solely to unearth

further stones. A borrowed roller was applied until the land was ready for the big moment.

George Scott gave me the seed.

'You don't want lawn seed for out there. I'll give you coarse grass seed.'

Carefully sowing, broadcast so that none fell by the wayside, I sang as I sowed as the starlings waited with open beaks. The evening sun mellowed the walls of the castle, the lowing herd wound slowly o'er the lee and I looked at the world, and the nearby churchyard and said to myself, 'Soul, take thine ease.'

Ten days later, after shower and rain, Billy Elliott came in with the milk.

'Vicar, can I bring a couple of sheep to graze where you have sown?'

With delight I asked, 'Is it up?'

'Aye, all green and plenty, but . . .'

'But me no buts', I quoted and ran out to see.

There, as a result of my tears, sweat and toil was a beautiful green carpet of young turnips!

Hide and Seek

All the birds of the air fell a-sighing and a-sobbing
  When they heard of the death of poor Cock Robin.
'Who'll dig his grave?'
'I', said the owl, 'with my spade and trowel;
  I'll dig his grave.'

I had no one to volunteer, as had the owl, to dig the grave of the grave-digger. Old Jack, verger and sexton, came to his last spadeful at the age of eighty-three. I had met this problem earlier at Bishopton where I had found the sexton dead in a grave that he was digging. We had no deputy at Mitford and no volunteer. My son, Paul, was an accountant and I reckoned that if the proposition was made to him in terms of finance we may get a conscript. Unused to manual labour, but being in a semi-permanent state of penury, he agreed to dig Jack's grave.

'How far do I go down, Dad?'

'As far as you can until it either caves in on you, or you come to an already present occupant.'

In the old part of the churchyard we had to dig them out to put them in! Early in the morning with the dew drenching the turf, Paul began his task. Dressed in old trousers and a black and white football shirt he began to prepare the narrow bed. The sun was shrinking when he reached the five foot level. Public interest had lured sightseers, including Dougie, the RAC man. They stood tottering on the brink of the excavation as Paul sweated and toiled and played to the gallery. Suddenly on the pointed end of his spade was a bone; a human arm bone. His reflex action threw the bone from the grave. Paul was petrified; Mac, my dog, delighted. The RAC recovery plan sprang into action. Mac dodged between the headstones and Dougie pursued him seeking to put a spanner in his works and we tried to head the dog away from the exits. Paul was left in the depths, straddling the recumbent incumbent of that narrow plot until the doctor, curious at the Olympics that were occurring in the hallowed acre, hove to alongside the grave. As he arrived there so did the forearm. The doctor looked at it and made the diagnosis,

'This fellow suffered from arthritis. See those red spots about the elbow, that's it.'

Old Tom replied, 'I'll be like the Pink Panther when I get to that stage. My joints fair murder me.'

We all gazed downwards.

'What have I to do, Dad?'

'What ever you do,' answered the RAC man, 'Don't disturb the skull. If you do you'll be haunted tonight.'

Dougie crossed his fingers, spat over his left shoulder and went in search of broken-down motorists. I deemed the grave deep enough, reckoned that Jack would never be lonely down there, and sprinkled a light disguising covering of soil over the remains. Paul slept uncertainly that night for he was certain that he had moved the skull.

The Innocents

The hospital was the happiest sphere in my parish. Allegedly it housed the mentally subnormal. I never used the term 'mentally subnormal' for, to me, it is either meaningless or applies to everyone. In all my naval and civilian experience I have never met normality, nor as a Christian have I looked for it. What is the criterion for normality? We are bound together as one in Christ, children of God, but at the same time we possess God's great gift to us; individuality. No one is exactly duplicated, not even identical twins, and I write as a twin. What may appear to be normal to some is regarded as abnormal by others. I do not accept the alternative term of 'mentally handicapped', for I believe that everyone has some form of mental handicap. I have studied and taught theology and can engage in a high standard of theological discussion, yet my handicap is mathematics. I can learn languages without any difficulty, but find a great handicap in speaking them. One can be a genius, filled with a broad spectrum of knowledge, yet, despite expertise, be utterly insensible to the sufferings and tribulations of others, and therefore incapable of sympathetic understanding. There are those who are capable of quick, academic achievement and yet in their human relationships be devoid of love. St. Paul recognised this when he wrote 'Though I have all knowledge and have not love, I am nothing.'

So, we tread an uncertain, and sometimes cruel, path if we employ the twin terms of 'sub-normal' and 'mentally handicapped'. In fact, from my experience at the hospital I have learnt to place great regard in the judgements and the attitudes of the patients, for, unlike alleged normal people, they have no guile or envy. I preferred to think of the population of the hospital as 'residents' who had been taken into care.

If I felt depressed or bewildered I would visit my friends in the hospital. All that they looked for was friendship and in return gave their devotion. Bishop Ashdown, on a visit to the

hospital, asked a group of patients what they thought of the staff 'and your vicar'. The reply came,
'Mr Richardson is not one of the staff; he's one of us.'

I never preached to them. Instead I involved them in discussion, for their capacity to concentrate was very limited. It was the twelfth Sunday after Trinity, known as Ephatha Sunday. Healing one who was deaf, Jesus used the Aramiac word to effect the healing, which, being interpreted means 'be opened'. I began by explaining to them what I would call 'odd words'.

'When all is well we say that it is OK; we say Cheerio when we mean Goodbye; and Cheers as we raise our drinks. Here's a funny word; Slangivar (Slainte Mor). It's used in Scotland instead of saying Cheers. Let's all say it.'

Then I made my great error.
I asked, 'Do you know any strange words?'
I spent years in the Navy and grew accustomed to the vocabulary of the messdeck, but the words the residents threw at me with great gusto and eagerness went beyond any imaginings of mine. Mary, the organist, played discord for the rest of the service.

It was St. John the Baptist day. I explained that it was the custom of the Jews to name the first born son after his father, intending to relate the variation in the case of John, whose father was Zacharias.

'Is there anyone here who has the same name as their father?'
Eight men and one woman indicated by raising their hands. I dealt with the Tommys, Bobbys, Jims and Jacks and then looked at Lucy.
'Now Lucy, how can you be named after your dad? Was he called Lucian?'
The congregation roared with laughter but eventually Lucy was able to speak. She is about fifty years of age, rotund with a wide beam, and wears her spectacles half-way down her nose. As she looks over them she speaks with a low, determined voice, and always precedes her conversation with 'I have news for you.'
Now she fixed me in focus over the top of her lenses and in

a stentorean boom declared

'Mr Richardson, I have news for you. My father's name was Alfred.'

The congregation burst into laughter. But undeterred Lucy continued,

'And my name is Lucy Alfreda Cox.'

John Brotherton is a joy to any chaplain. He is an ever-present member of the congregation, be the service on Sunday or weekday. He lives and breathes religion. Fearlessly he declares that Jesus should be the hammer of trade unions, that shop assistants were godless as they took money for the goods, and it is hard for rich people to enter heaven, his own undisputed destination and mine too if entry depends upon poverty.

In the summer weeks he still goes on Saturday evenings to nearby Morpeth to listen to blood and thunder being brimstoned liberally from the wayside pulpits. On the following Sunday mornings I was the conscripted recipient of resumés of the tirades, and my opinions bore great weight with John.

His one ambition was to inherit the Kingdom of Heaven and he was spiritually and physically disturbed when he feared that he may unwittingly be barred from the apocalyptic delights. He had spent a restless night pondering his quandary as he pounded regularly between his bed and the lavatory. His bowels clarified his decision to come to me.

'Will you arrange for me to have a blood test?'

'A blood test John? That's not for me to arrange. If you need one you must consult your charge nurse and he'll arrange with Dr Gwyn Williams for you to go to the treatment centre. Anyway, why do you want a blood test?'

'Well, Mr Richardson, it's like this. The preacher at Morpeth said last night that it is only by the blood of Jesus that we are saved. I want to be sure that I'm in the right blood group.'

I lifted his eyelid, peered into that perplexed optic and assured him that he was saved. I had done something. He had both felt me and seen me do it. He was satisfied with my verdict, no doubt regarding me as being in the same union as

Jesus. Unfortunately, I had opened the gates of heaven for many for I had to inspect the eyes of all witnesses, as God is no respecter of persons; and it looks as if St. Peter will have to revise his signs, symbols and tokens and admit all who give the glad-eye.

In all my years at the hospital I did not encounter, or hear of any act of cruelty or violence by the staff against the patients. The staff, without exception, are dedicated men and women who genuinely strive for the well-being of those committed to their care. Of course, there has to be discipline and at times punishment, as a loving father has to chastise his own children. There are times too, when, because of the nature of their malady, some patients develop periods of violence and, for their own safety and that of their companions, have to be restricted for a little while. Carol was a lovely girl both in features and personality. She was over six feet tall and extremely lean and lanky. She loved to sing in church although it was obvious as she shattered the eardrums of all about her, that she was completely tone-deaf.

The nursing staff recognised the symptoms of violence developing from Carol's depression, but Carol precipitated action by suddenly thrusting her fist through a window pane, almost severing her artery. So she was placed in a room by herself. Apart from a bed without blankets or sheets, there were no furnishings at all upon which she could inflict injury upon herself. She was without clothing, as that too could have been a weapon of self destruction. Her toilet arrangements were looked after by the staff, who escorted her, clad in a cordless dressing gown, to the necessary ablutions. She ranted and raved for a space of three days, then began to improve. She was allowed a visit from her friend, a plump, jolly patient from the same ward. Together they hatched up an escape plan.

I had been visiting a parishioner who lived near the hospital. With all the time in the world at my disposal I drove slowly back toward the Vicarage. Workmen were busy at the northern end of the newly constructed bypass which coincided with the road into the hospital. I saw Carol standing at the roadside, dressed in a loose blouse and short skirt. I knew that she should not have been there, so as I slackened pace I decided to take her back to the ward. Suddenly she flung herself in front of my car. The wheels rolled her to one side. I stopped and leapt out but she was up and legging it as fast as she could in the wrong direction. I ran after her. Her legs could outstride mine easily and I realised that she would get away unless I flung myself at her in a rugby style tackle. In a glorious assault my arms triumphantly met about her waist and we both fell to the ground. Unfortunately, as she fell my grip dislodged the skirt from her hips and she was completely naked from the waist down. A passing lorry driver, seeing a young girl apparently being sexually assaulted by a man wearing a dog-collar, slowed up and called out,

'You filthy bastard,' but did not come to the girl's assistance.

Carol was almost instantly on her feet again, her lanky unclad legs haring it towards distant Scotland. I called to the workmen who had been at least interested spectators and they joined me in the chase. Three men sat on her as I went to bring my car to convey her to the hospital. Her struggle had the strength of unrestricted mania and the workmen lost the battle.

The foreman said to me, 'I wouldn't put her in the car; she'll tear it to bits.'

Just then a miracle happened and a great calm came upon us. Carol noticed one of her captives and fell in an immediate, instant love with him. He was seventeen and already terribly embarrassed. She ceased her struggles with us but went into a determined love huddle with the youth, kissing and mauling him like a lioness in season.

Above her muffled declarations of love I yelled, 'Put them both into the back of the car.'

The reluctant swain, with Carol sticking to him like a leech, was bundled into the car and I drove quickly into the hospital grounds. A search party had been scouring the precincts, and they met me and relieved me of the unashamed and half naked lover girl. I told the lad to wait a moment and I would drive him back to his work but he didn't wait and performed a neat hurdle over a gate and disappeared.

Carol was back in church the next Sunday with no recollection of her Godiva dash. Her friend had arranged to leave clothing in the toilet for Carol, and she had escaped by squeezing through a very small window. The girl had sacrificed her own clothing for Carol, but she was a forty-five inch waist, hence the dislodged skirt.·

John Brotherton never removed his hat from his head when in church. Perhaps it was a mark of respect that its peak was turned towards heaven. With his skyward peak he told me that his friend Bob had gone to heaven. All of John's friends eventually go to heaven. I hope the system does not change for I am one of John's friends. So it came about that John was asked to remove his cap when in the crematorium for Bob Cook's tour. A shocked John refused to remove it, and I don't know whether it was foresight or judgement on John's part, for when I manipulated the little lever which signals the committal to the elements, nothing happened. The coffin remained still as if in a lay-by. I desperately worked the lever in every possible direction even though I knew that it simply operated a little red light beyond the curtain. I began to think that perhaps the burner-upper was delayed on natural requisites, or engrossed in the *Sporting Journal,* when it happened.

The congregation consisted of twelve patients, one male nurse and the undertaker. John's eyes followed the direction of his cap peak when a cloud of smoke particles belched forth from behind the curtain. Bits of debris fell everywhere.

The vestry door behind me opened.

'Get them out Jack, the place is on fire.'

Not wishing to stampede the patients I said,

'Let us pray,' to which John replied 'Amen'.

We said the Lord's prayer and through the chaos and smoke as if from Mount Sinai, I pronounced a blessing. Quietly I walked to the main door and shook hands with the patients as they left. They thought the explosion was the normal process of cremation and were not bothered. As soon as the last mourner had left, I hurried behind the scenes. There was devastation. Bits of coffin and residue scattered the floor. The superintendent told me on my next visit that the body awaiting cremation before Bob's was so full of gasses that when it went into the burning fiery furnace it had blown up.

Maureen was incurably blind. I know nothing of anatomy or our nervous system but speaking in layman's terms, there was no means of communication from Maureen's dark and attractive eyes to her brain. She was born with a handicap and because of it she was rejected by her parents. She was a lovely girl in every way; her personality oozed with energy and joy. She lived in perpetual darkness. She was quick to learn her whereabouts and the furnishings in her ward and dormitory were always most carefully arranged in their original positions. Once she had the confidence of her surroundings she could run and walk about with assurance of other children. She could find her pew in church without any guidance. I had long chats with her and told her of the teeming activities of nature. I could explain to her the warmth of the sun upon her cheeks, or the chilling grip of winter's blasts and the winds and breezes. I stood with her on the leafy banks of the Wansbeck as she first dipped her fingers into the gentle current and then, removing her socks and shoes, stepped into the shallow water. So she learnt of fish and streams, of birds and flowers and of God's purpose in creation. How she imagined them I cannot tell, but she had a mind curious to enquire and quick to assimilate.

I went into her ward after school hours. She came bounding down the clear corridor at a rate of knots, bubbling over with excitement. She pulled me into the day-room and flung her excited arms unerringly around my neck.
'I'm going to see; I'm going to see; like you and everybody else. I'll see everything!'

The words tumbled out in a cascade of ecstasy. Eventually, she calmed down to tell me of her hopes. Some well-meaning but misguided, evangelist paying a one-off visit, had told the children of the healing miracles of Jesus. After the story of the restorations of sight to the blind man it was natural for Maureen to ask, 'Will Jesus give me sight?'
'Of course he will; if you keep on saying your prayers and believe. You will get your sight'.

Maureen said to me, 'I have said my prayers more than ever, and I know that God will hear your prayers because you are a vicar; so will you pray for me now?'

Tears blinded my eyes. Her keen, upturned face with its sightless eyes, beautiful in its childlike trust, tormented me. I was pleased that she could not see my emotion. I longed to take her into my arms and say 'Yes, yes, you will see soon', but I knew the answer. I prayed indeed but it was that Maureen may have the strength and guidance to help her accept the bitter disappointment that would follow this false hope. It took weeks and gently but surely God helped both Maureen and me. She left us when she was fourteen to go to a school for the blind, knowing that she possessed the light and vision of a simple trusting faith. She could see perhaps far better than many sighted people, the like of whom Jesus said 'They look but do not see; they hear but do not understand'.

Leeks

'Any other business?' enquired the Parish Council Chairman.

The agenda had been concerned with the aromas from pigsties, which were adding spice to the bar lunches, broken fences which allowed cattle to endanger leek trenches, which is the cardinal sin, rubbish dumping in the river, football on the village green and the details of events for the forthcoming Queen's Silver Jubilee.

'Aye', said Bill Elliott, 'I have some further business'.

He coughed and apologised, 'Sorry, I have a sore throat'.

'I'm sucking a throat tablet', I said, 'Would you like a suck?'

'No thank you, Vicar. It's about the right-of-way across my land. Hoards of hikers use it, and as there are no toilets in the vicinity they use my stack of haybales. Sorry to say this in front of you Vicar, but to be blunt', here I trembled, 'I wouldn't mind too much if they only spent a penny, but they do five bob's worth. Then my sheep roll in it. Only tonight before I came here I tossed two dogs in the river to cleanse them. Could the path be diverted?'

One caught the picture of an army of incontinent athletic ramblers invading the place, when, in fact, the odd wayfarer trod this pilgrim's way. For hundreds of years it had been trodden by the feet of pious pilgrims seeking healing at Holy Well. A full discussion followed and I ventured, timorously, that the solution might lie in the re-siting of the haystack.

At this point, just as George Brown, the chairman, was about to relate the lurid stories of courting days down by that right-of-way, a man intruded. He was not simply a man but a member of that elite body, the Leek Club Committee.

'Is this the leek club meeting?' he asked.

'No', said Geordie, 'that's in the Plough. Hang on and I'll come with you.'

George was chairman of that too.

The Leek Club Committee, of which I was then secretary,

being the member who could write, went into earnest session, for Sim Henderson wished to discuss a serious rumour that was circulating. It concerned a diabolical threat, originating in Mitford, of women forming a Leek Club. When Sim first broached the subject there was a thunder of unbelieving utterances, and pints and half pints were spilled down shirt fronts and T-shirts. Sim's eloquence was encouraged by the sceptical attention his message received, and he warmed to his subject reaching a climax by demanding that as far as leek clubs were concerned they were 'no-go' areas for the weaker sex. Sanctions and restrictions upon the women were suggested and even sabotage — if the idea ever got off the ground or rather into the ground — but the prohibition of sexual activity received no support and was only a tentative suggestion by Andy who was a bachelor.

The leek club world is like a two-sided coin. On one side there is patient, earnest endeavour and perseverance. There is challenge and the fruits of conquest. On the other there is the dark side of intrigue, falsehoods, exaggerations and cloak and dagger activities that would shame the Mafia. In this scientific age, leek-slashing has been replaced by weedkiller sprays and electronic devices. I had an advantage for I could pray for a localized blight upon my opponents' trenches!

Flags, buttons and beards may sound like references to outings for old men but they belong to the vocabulary of the leek men. Not only did I, as an initiate, have to learn and understand these terms, but I had to recognise the red-herrings that were as plentiful as the leeks.

'I'm having difficulty getting any plants this year.'

'There's a shortage. I'll have to make do with poor seed.'

'Red rust has decimated my leeks', was a common exaggeration.

'I think I'll have to miss the show this year'. And so it went on.

Yet, when I made my pastoral visits to the homes of the leek growers I was carefully shepherded in through the front doors and taken into the front parlours so that I couldn't see the giant oaks which were thriving so splendidly in their back gardens!

'I'll have a look at your leeks before I go Isaac.'

'Oh no, the back door's jammed. Have to get it seen to.'

One or two members seeking spiritual favours or with pregnant wives would counsel me.

'Put them in North and South.'

'Divvent put them in too deep.'

'Put them well doon' and,

'Divvent watter them.'

I received advice on how to get rid of slugs, blights, wet-rot, cats and other insidious destroyers such as the members themselves.

I stuck my plants in the ground and prayed. They drooped like sea grass after the tide had left them. All the conniving members who made excuses to see them assured me that they were winners. By God's providence and healthy manure and a little bonemeal from the churchyard, my leeks prospered. The great day came!

Billy Holmes dug them up for me, and gave me this advice, 'First, always wash your leeks in the rain or river water, never tap water.'

Accordingly I went riverwards carrying two pails. The early morning mists still swirled around the spectral bodies of Bill Cuthbert's cows as I stumbled along the river bank. I filled two pails with water but found it extremely difficult to ascend to level ground bearing overflowing buckets. Again and again I spilled it until finally, with water-logged shoes and sodden socks, I won the day. Fuller's Earth could not have been more effective. My leeks gleamed whiter than white.

The second piece of advice came from Billy Elliott the milk-man,

'Rub the flags with the top of the milk'.

I had ordered three extra pints and Ethel administered the lotion which really had an amazing effect. Still further advice came from Ronnie Hopper who grew no leeks but advised everyone,

'Comb the beards'.

Comb them! Where could I obtain a comb? The parting in my hair is four inches wide. I remembered that a long-haired bridegroom had left a comb in the vestry. The transformation was complete and I loaded them into the car, stuck a sign in my rear window declaring Long Load and departed for the Televiewers' Hut.

On the way home I saw Isaac carefully shielding his precious burden from the warm, withering rays of the sun as, he too, trod the path to the hut. His treasures were snuggly wrapped in swaddling bands against the rude and enquiring glances of others. His step was careful and measured lest any jerk should bruise or scar his load. I pulled up, although he would have wished me to ignore him. I hailed him boisterously and in a hoarse whisper he begged me to modulate my voice to a more ecclesiastical murmur. After much persuasion he allowed my gaze to fall upon the objects of his love. Beneath the safe wrappings, their once tousled heads lying neat and uniform and with white tapes about their loins, lay, not his grandbairns but his leeks. Torturous weeks of worry, of careful nourishing, of wife-neglect and watchful nights were about to culminate in, he hoped, a great reward. Now on his way to the leek show he had met the parson. Surely this was a Divine omen. So he implored me to invoke a blessing upon his leeks. Hurriedly endeavouring to recall all the special prayers and intercessions I had used from 'Short prayers for single people', 'Thanksgiving of women after childbirth' to 'Prayers for a launch' I managed to revive a Druidic benediction and pronounced it over his leeks. Confident now that all was won, with a lighter step and the first prize practically in his pocket, Isaac sailed forth to the Televiewers' Hut that had never seen a television.

Time dragged on leaden feet. A steady procession of leek enthusiasts delivered their entries to the hut and waited in the Plough. Billy Ross was running a book on the show and Geordie Brown was the odds-on favourite to win. He had carried his leeks like fallen oaks from his timber yard as another competitor derided him, crying,

'What's them? Scallions?'

George was equal to him, though, and replied, 'You should see the ones I've left in the trench'.

The last moment of the First Dog Watch meandered by and took with it the nerve-wracking suspense of the competitors. All was now to be revealed. Those who had put money on Geordie had squandered it, for Old Jack Thompson had won and had beaten the aforesaid scallions into second place. Jack's effort contained twenty-three cubic inches, and he could now pass his declining years with Martha happily knowing Paradise had reached down to earth for him that day.

Where were the blessed leeks of Isaac? Rejected by the judge for being an eighth of an inch too long!

Sunset

A few acres clung around the dwelling place. I cannot call it a house. It had grown up years ago and long before the days of planning permits and council restrictions. There must have been a succession of eccentric occupants who had all shared the desire not to encroach upon the land of their small-holding, for the building barely touched the ground, while it structured towards the ample acres of sky like a grotesque finger crippled with arthritis. Andy's complaint was not arthritis but an incurable longing to imbibe. He was pickled in alcohol. Like most alcoholics he was a pleasant and generous man but he stood only five feet tall. He lived in one room. The rest of the house was a mystery except to the little creatures of the wild that had easy access through tiny broken and irregular windows. Andy never bothered with a carpet, lino or rushes, but kept a plentiful supply of newspapers on the deck. By the door was a plastic sack.

Nestling against the south-west wall was his leek trench. Contrasting with the living room it was neat, orderly and well tended. The best fertilizers rotted beneath the richness of the topsoil. Seaweed, painstakingly matured liquid manure and the seasoned droppings from his solitary cow rotted away among the bodies of dead dogs and cows. It was said that Andy's highest placement in the leek show was the year he nurtured his precious plants in the bowels of an old ewe.

The gaunt skeleton of a permanently leafless tree outside his door could not denote the season, but in the distance rooks cawed over the trees, which were beginning to don their russet hues. It was September. Andy stood with a warm breeze drifting his breath and desires towards the Plough, when he had a stroke. He recovered consciousness in the unfamiliar, clinical cleanliness of the Cottage Hospital. I visited him.

The matron spoke over the phone,
'Vicar, could you come this afternoon and visit Andy? He says that he's going to die tonight and in his present state of mind he will. The doctor can find nothing wrong with him. In fact he seems to be improving, but seems determined to die. Come and talk to him'.
I sat at his bedside. He gazed into a void until my voice penetrated, chasing away all his visions of whisky galore.
'Hey Andy. I hear tell you're going to die tonight.'
He just grunted his concurrence.

119

'You can't die tonight Andy. It's the leek show on Saturday'.
Again he grunted.
'Yes, you may well grunt. I would if I had leeks like yours.
You haven't a chance.'
Immediately he spoke. 'They're better than yours.'
'No way', I teased, 'They're no better than spring onions'.
Indignantly he declared, 'They'll beat yours'.
'Andy?' I spoke slowly and deliberately, 'They cannot beat
anybody's, for they'll not be in the show. We don't accept
dead men's leeks'.
There was a profound silence. Andy was thinking and his
momentous decision was spoken with a firm resolve.
'I'll hang on'.
After agreeing to wager for half a bottle of whisky, I left Andy
invoking the Gods for his survival.

The judge, fearing that his verdict might have eternal
repercussions, placed Andy's leeks at nineteenth and my
lordly leeks stood at twentieth. I rang the matron.
'Cheer Andy up and tell him that he's won the whisky. I'll be
in on Monday to see him.'

Andy's eyes went straight to the wrapped bottle in my
hand and I saw the twin virtues of desire and satisfaction in
those searching optics.
'What did I win?' asked Andy, propped up against his
pillows.
'A pair of sheets', I informed him.
And he answered with a flash of humour, 'They'll do to lay
me out with!'

He never drank the whisky. I was summoned hastily to the
hospital just after tea. Andy was letting go his grip. In pain he
cried pitifully. His face was distorted and purple. His eyes
started from their sockets and he gasped between his shouts. I
shouted the Communion service. Then a miracle happened. I
saw the peace of God. Although his voice drowned mine I
quietly pronounced,
'The peace of God which passes all understanding, keep your
heart and mind . . .'
As I spoke, a calm radiance spread over those tortured

features. His eyes grew soft and easy; his breathing was no longer laboured. I could see the assurance that comes from peace of mind spread over him. After a silence that may have lasted an age or just a second Andy smiled at me and took my hand.

'Let's say the Lord's prayer again', he requested.

Never at any time has that lovely prayer had a deeper meaning than it had then. Through the window we could see the westering sun bringing the glory of heaven through the clouds above the wide greenness of the golf course. The glory was reflected in Andy's face as he said to me without any note of sadness,

'I'll be on the other side of that sunset before dark'.

I took his hand. He did not relax his grip until looking at me from above and through the slanting rays of the sun he said 'Goodbye'.

The whisky was consumed at his funeral. He would have liked it that way!

As I turned from his graveside I felt a touch on my shoulder.

'Vicar, is there any chance of getting Andy's place in the leek club?'

Life and leeks go on.

Savile Row

I had been requested to preach 'a short sermon'. It was to be delivered from the stage of a dance hall. No robes were to be worn. I stood in my best grey suit, a new clerical collar encircled my neck and my clerical garb was completed by a pectoral cross. My mind nervously grappled with the problem of how to exercise the correct etiquette in greeting the eminent personage about to enter through the ballroom doors. Should I bow, kiss his hand and swoon or simply scream and applaud? My indecision grew to utter bewilderment when the door opened and in he came, bestowing his blessings and cigar smoke upon me. His flowing locks curled in contemptuous confusion from his shoulders in a heavenward direction. The smoke of his cigar lazily lingered like a lost halo about his pointed shoes, so daintily dented. Like two scarlet-corded arrows his legs met the shoes but were obscured from the knees waistward by a three-quarter mandarin jacket of bright floral design. Beneath the open jacket there screamed a salmon-shaped high necked tunic and about his neck there hung, in gay profusion, a medley of necklaces and chains. From the chains there tinkled or clanged a motley carillon of cowbells, bringing with them the suggestion of the Swiss Alps or a herd of Maltese goats. The whole was crowned with a superb wreath of knee length flowers in cream and green.

With a 180 degrees bow he greeted me, 'Good morning, your Lordship', and my day was made.

Was he an Eastern potentate? One of the hierarchy of an Eastern Orthodox church or from a way-out political conference? He was much more than all of these. From this day I was to respect and admire the man, for not only was his appearance unforgettable but so was his presence and his sermon. He was Jimmy Savile.

122

He faced the leaders and organisers of the Youth March which had earlier taken place in Newcastle, a march that had been designed to show to the general public that the majority of our youngsters today, are not drug addicts. They marched to oppose any legislation that would make it easier, or even seem respectable, to obtain drugs. These clear-minded youngsters had marched to the Lord Mayor of Newcastle to present a petition objecting to a proposed Bill, about to be laid before Parliament, that would make the purchase of drugs possible over the counters of chemists' shops easier and even legal.

One of my parishioners, Bill Leech, was so impressed by their courage and example that he gave the youngsters silver mementoes of the march.

I was to say a few prayers and give a few words. Then Jimmy spoke. With rare genius and direct, unyielding approach, this idol of the Pop world held us all enthralled as he spoke of the dangers and destructive potentialities of drug taking. Warming to the crux of his sermon, which was absolutely extemporary, he spoke with fervent faith in God.

Referring to drugs he said, 'We don't need a chemical crutch. Use God as your crutch. Lean on Him. He will not let you down or suffer to see you slide.'

'There is no way of escape, certainly drugs don't provide one, other than God. He will, and does provide the way of escape which does not cloak or disguise reality, but gives the strength, courage and determination to face, meet and conquer outward adversities. Set God firmly in your minds. That will give you direction, show you purpose and lighten your load. Try it. I have. It works'.

Bella

Bella was one month short of a hundred years when she died. She was over ninety when she had a special visitor. Her home was spotless. Every morning she had dismantled her fireplace, cleaned the flues, replaced them and kindled her fire before six o'clock. Her coal shovel handle was daily scrubbed and the dust blown from the coal before it was brought into the house. Under five feet in height this little spindle of energy was tough and wiry. She would carry a bucket of hot water and a scrubbing brush half a mile to the churchyard every month to clean her parents' headstone. She was so independent that she spurned my offer to do it for her, or at least to supply the water and bucket. The longest journey she had ever made in her life, until they took her to a home in Ashington, was the four miles from her home in Pigdon to the market town of Morpeth. Her father, who also lived to be over ninety, had been a farm worker and he reared his family on the princely wage of ten shillings each week and permission to keep a cow. The cow was kept in a field, which to this day is known as Buddle's Field. Bella as a girl, got out of bed at six o'clock every morning to collect the cow and milk it before setting off on the three mile hike to school at Mitford.

She had never seen a colour magazine, a television or colour photographs. She had a small radio and listened to the daily service and very little more. She was most devout and as long as her short legs would carry her she walked every Sunday down and then up the steep hill to church.

Removing unsightly weeds from her garden she cut her heel. It refused to heal. Her doctor was afraid that the wound might become gangrenous so he arranged daily visits by the district nurse, to have the heel cleansed and dressed. Bella loved this! She was receiving more attention now than she had ever enjoyed before. By the time the nurse arrived every morning, Bella had prepared a tray with two cups, her mother's flowered teapot which was a hundred years old, and a plate of biscuits. The nurse made Bella feel that she was the most important patient on her list and a happy friendship ensued.

One Saturday morning the nurse informed Bella,
'I won't be coming for the next two weeks. I'm going on

holiday, but I've arranged for a relief nurse to look after you. I don't know which one it will be yet but she'll come at the same time as I've been coming and I am sure that she'll appreciate a cup of tea.'

Monday, mid-morning, saw Bella standing by her neatly arranged tray, dressed in her usual ankle length dress, covered by a spotless pinafore. She wore only one stocking in preparation for the nurse's medical attention. The door resounded to the resolute pounding of the nurse who had evidently been informed of Bella's dull hearing. Bella hobbled slowly to the door, opened it, and within ten seconds had barricaded herself in her bedroom and wedged herself beneath her bed! The nurse followed her to the now bolted bedroom door and spoke but was answered only by low sobs and moans.

A neighbour's help proved ineffective and they went for Geordie Brown. He talked through the bastion of the solid door but Bella insisted that she talk to the Vicar. I got in. She told me that she must have committed some terrible sin in her life, of which she was not aware, but which had caused the Devil himself to come for her soul.

'I opened the door and there he stood; the Devil.'

The poor soul was terrified and all because she had not been told that the relief nurse was coloured. In fact, the nurse was an Abyssinian and very black. Bella had never set eyes on a coloured person in her life. Eventually I persuaded Bella to come into the living room, where she sat on the other side of the table to the nurse but with her head turned away. The nurse brewed the tea.

Bella kept giving her sly glances until the nurse extended her arm towards her.

'Look, the palm of my hand is as white as yours.'

Bella no doubt believing that no part of the Devil could be white studied the palm then touched it, and, licking her finger, tried to erase the colour from the back of the hand. Contact had been made. Bella grew bold. She asked if the nurse's close crop of jet-black curls were real and the nurse invited her to pull them. The almost scalped nurse survived and to Bella she was transformed from his Satanic Majesty to an angel of mercy. In her blunt Northumbrian way Bella never ceased to relate afterwards that she had a friend who was a 'Blackie'.

Hurtling Hearse

'The terminal has fallen.'
Jack Thompson's terminology conveyed the possibility of snow. He needed no barometer. His aches and pains occasioned by his stealthy stoops over his leek trench indicated what climatic condition we were to expect. In accordance with, and maybe because of, Jack's observations, the skies grew leaden and daylight turned to mid-day dusk. A quietness muffled the sounds of nature. The first snow flakes fluttered down as if reluctant to meet the impeding earth. The sun was absent and the air keen. The 'terminal' had certainly fallen.

The Farmers' Union thought that if it obtained the services of a cleric as after-dinner speaker at its annual feed-up, it would ensure that next year's harvest would be bountiful. So it was that I looked at the sky, and Jack Thompson's receding and buckled back, and decided to get to Seahouses before the roads became treacherous. As I drove the snow intensified and drifted before the driving wind, but I arrived at my destination at tea time, three and a half hours too soon for the meal with the farmers. Jack Britton was a kindly, jovial fellow and his wife an excellent cook. His house was on the coast, the snow pelted upon me like salted potato crisps, as I knocked in expectation of a generous welcome. Jack and his wife had known me for many years and soon I was sitting in his lounge before a warming fire, eating home-baked, waist-destroying scones and buns.

I was reluctant to leave Jack's hospitality to walk to his restaurant where the farmers were to further enlarge their corpulence. Little did I, or anyone else, realise that this was the last time I would ever have tea with Jack.

Jim Manners had supplied the beef and Jim was an expert on meat. The succulent roast added taste to the Yorkshire puddings, and sank deliciously to swim in an ocean of spirit lubrication, which lined our innards. To make sure that the well-being spirit did not dry up there was a liberal supply and choice of wines. It was all food and fellowship within. All was drastically antarctic without. The trousers of the farmers with ample pockets to accommodate their brass, tightened about the equators of their waists as they did justice to Mrs Britton's cooking, and the snow outside heightened to the window ledges. They had endured my exposition when a coastguard came in.

'All roads from Seahouses are blocked. Anyone living more than six miles away is stuck here. Make mine a double brandy.'

Grace Darling's ghost must have been on watch over the Farnes for the coastguard had settled in for the night and he was dedicated to making a tide of alcohol disappear.

Jim Manners beaming benevolence said, in a rash moment, 'Jack you'll have to spend the night at my house. I'll phone Nancy'.

So seven men of merriment disturbed the peace of Preston Main. With good judgement Nancy Manners had left the decanters at the ready and had retired for the night. It was well past midnight but Jim's extended hospitality knew no restricting hours, and it was near to four o'clock when I extinguished my bedroom light and went out like a light myself.

The sizzling of bacon accompanied Jim's intrusion and message that breakfast was ready.

'There's a razor in the bathroom. Don't be long.'

Jim weighed in at over sixteen stone and I am a mere stripling of eleven stone. I tripped as I walked in his pyjamas. They fell about my feet and I scurried unclad to the refuge of the bathroom. It was as large as a stable and the toothbrush looked as if it belonged to a horse. I used it with carbolic soap.

The electric razor may have been left behind by Hawkeye for it tore, tugged and plucked at my beard leaving me like the last of the Mohicans.

Grapefruit, followed by bacon, eggs, sausage, tomatoes, fried bread, toast, and marmalade with steaming mugs of coffee chased away the hangover of the previous night. I was welcome to stay the weekend but the next day would be the Sabbath and I had been informed by phone that a funeral had been arranged for Monday. It took me little less than an hour to reach the main arterial road even though it was only three miles distant.

I plodded my way through the snowdrifts to the church boiler house. The steps had become a ski slope and I hit every rib as I plunged my involuntary descent. The boiler house door had stood open and the snow had changed its colour as it had drifted in. I switched the boiler on and scaled up to ground level. After a warming cup of cocoa I searched out the portable snowplough George Brown had made for the churchyard from a discarded laying-out board for the dead. I puffed and panted up and down the churchyard paths pushing the snow towards the graves. I heard no voice of complaint.

A screeching owl from the four hundred year old American redwood told the snow desert that another day had ended. The moon was losing its grey halo as I struggled through the darkened hallowed acre to check on the boiler. Headstones watched like white shrouded wraiths as I plumbed the sepulchral depths of the boiler house. It was as cold as a mortuary. There is no desolation like a defunct boiler. I began my inspection of feeds, fuels and pipes and set about to try to remedy the faults. The task was beyond me. The thermostat, oil and water were all frozen. I worked until nine o'clock and in the end prayed that the snow would block the road to the church.

Sunday morning did not dawn. Icicles hung from the castle walls and from the organ chamber in the church. The organist didn't make it either. No solemn summons sounded over the silent village to alert its sleeping populace to the hour of prayer as the bells were as frozen as the proverbial monkeys. Olive Witt, in seaboots and woollies, with a prayful piety and painful persistence pioneered a path to church, a path soon obliterated and only disturbed again as the same lady, reinforced spiritually but physically so chilled as to be insensible to pain, did a Matterhorn homewards. It was the beginning of the hard, long winter of 1982.

The funeral was timed for ten thirty on Monday morning. Mrs Dobson had asked me, when in hospital, if she would get home for Christmas. She did, as I assured her that she would, but it was a home where chills of winter would no longer blast beneath the portals. I hope that her great sense of humour lived on, for she would enjoy the comedy of sequences which attended her funeral.

The phone rang. Archie Campbell, the volunteer organist, a mere probationer of eighty six years, informed me that the water in his car radiator was frozen and asked me to go to Morpeth to collect him. It was nine thirty. Carefully I crossed the bridge. Beneath me was the frozen river Wansbeck and I skidded, fouling the far fence and running backwards until the car hit the ramparts of the bridge. The rear bumper was dislodged. Like Robert the Bruce I tried again and again to spider my way to the top.

I stood at the lych gate, wearing a sheepskin beneath my cassock and surplice. Ten thirty came but not the hearse. A few villagers had won through on foot and sat in the church like trussed turkeys in a deep freeze. Archie was playing Handel's Largo with woollen mitts adorning his hands and no-one cared if it sounded like the 'Skater's Waltz'. It was ten minutes to eleven o'clock when the hearse limped alongside the churchyard gate.

It looked like a gigantic Cyclops as one massive headlight hung sightless from its socket. The nearside wing was crumpled and the door buckled.

'What happened?' I enquired.

The undertaker was from the Co-op. He had a funereal glaze about his shrouded eyes. He sighed as he surveyed his vehicle and saw a drop in his dividend.

'It was your bank.'

If anything went wrong on the church hill it was 'my bank'. 'The brakes wouldn't hold the hearse and I crashed into the car ahead of me. It's a write off.'

'Whose was the other car?' I asked.

'Mine', he mournfully chattered, 'It was carrying the underbearers. We're late because we had to crowbar the wing out of the tyre.'

Anxiously I enquired if the stricken vessel would make it to the crematorium.

'Yes', he replied, 'But make this service short. Cut out the hymns and say nowt.'

Ten minutes later the slithering underbearers replaced the coffin in the one-eyed, geriatric conveyance and I climbed into the front seat of the first mourner's car. The hearse led the way about ten yards ahead of us. It navigated the bridge but came to grief again on the first brow of the hill. It ran backwards penetrating the hedge and coming to rest overhanging the icebound waters. The undertaker, our car driver and me tried to get the hearse back onto the road but we could not get behind it. A shovel and a pick were brought from the Vicarage and we hacked through the frozen surface to the hard earth beneath, then scattered soil about the wheels. Slowly, like a huge, clumsy, black slug it disentangled itself from the encircling hedge and we were able to get behind it and push. It progressed about four yards and then ran backwards again, its rear, off-side wheel running over me. I rolled down the hill and hit the kerbstone at the bottom. I sustained a dislocated shoulder, three cracked teeth, bruised ribs and a gashed knee. While dear old ladies fussed around me as I lay like a stricken crow in my black cassock, the hearse made it to the top. The car that I should have been in followed the hearse, but only succeeded by running its wheels deep in the hedge. This resulted in the passenger door becoming so distorted it could not open. The next car, a mustard coloured Granada, came to grief on the first brow and executed a 180 degree turn, ran down the hill and crashed into a little mini car and completely blocked the road. Like a weird figure from

Wuthering Heights.the black-clad undertaker gesticulated and shouted from the top of the hill demanding that I wasted no more time. Blood seeped through the knee of my trousers and my right hand hung helplessly by my side, but I reached the car. I had to enter through the driver's door and do a combat course over the gearstick and brake handle. I further tore my cassock.

It was ten minutes to one o'clock when we reached the crematorium. When I tried to lift my arm to commit the body to the elements, it refused to function and in my pain I whispered to Mrs Dobson, snug in her narrow mantle, 'Move along, bonny lass, I'll come with you'.

We set off for Mitford in the battered car. I longed to get back, but my longing was frustrated when we reached Morpeth. The fish and chip shop was on fire. Thick black fumes, completely hiding the buildings, caused me to wonder about the nature of the oil used in the processing of haddock and spuds. Hose pipes patterned the sodden highway and fire engines reflected on the greasy roads. Clouds of whitish foam were pumped into the building. Two things were obvious. There would be no frying that night and I was not going to reach home before the Morpeth curfew rang out from the ancient clock tower.

The car stopped at the top of the church hill.
'I'm not risking a journey down there. You'll have to walk. Here, take this with you and put it on Mr Dobson's grave.' With this the driver deposited a five foot cross of yellow roses upon my back. So I limped down the hill, one arm useless, the other clutching my surplice and scarf while endeavouring to balance the cross upon my back. I could have done with Simon of Cyrene.

I phoned the doctor, then the phone summoned me. Jovial Jim Manners was not jovial now. Sadly and deeply moved he told me Jack Britton had just been killed. He said Jack had been involved in a car crash and had died of a heart attack. I sat by the fire watching the flames consume a log, counting myself fortunate that my injuries were so light. I felt a tear for Jack course down my cheek. Although I had seen very little of him of late I was fond of him. He was a good man, a kind and a geniune, thinking Christian. I was still on the injured list on the day of his funeral but I went to my church and quietly remembered Jack.

The doctor came. He jerked my shoulder into position as I jumped almost to the ceiling. I went to bed. Again the phone jangled. I lifted it to hear the voice of one of my students. 'Vicar, will you marry me? I'm pregnant.'
So another day was ended and another step taken along the road of life.

The Quick and The Dead

The path was well worn to the crematorium. The service had been held in the chapel of Northgate Hospital and we now bore old Dora to her last, we hoped, inflagration. I sat in the front seat of the hearse between the driver and the undertaker. Behind us were three cars carrying mourners and the hospital mini-bus carrying patients. Several of the market day shoppers showed their respect by removing their headwear as we passed them by, through the small town to climb the Station Bank. Soon we were in the sylvan garden of Nedderton Village. As every Eden has its serpent, the very beauty of the countryside seemed to grow ominous as the serpent unwound itself, not from an apple tree, but from behind a telephone kiosk. Its deadly fang was a radar pistol and its markings were police-blue with a chequered crown. Our fallen nature was revealed.

'Thou shalt not eat up the way at more than thirty miles per hour'.

The fiery prophet of retribution rebuked us in stern judgement. We cast our minds about us. Had old Dora, encased in wood and delineated in brass and seemingly at peace behind us, beguiled us? As a daughter of Eve was she reluctant to leave this earthly sphere before she had caused the downfall of Adam, for our driver's name was Adam. The Law, wielding his flaming sword in the shape of the condemning gun, conducted his inquisition with an awesome majesty of a deity and the infallibility of the Bishop of Rome. Engraved upon his tablet was the damning evidence that the hearse had been galloping at thirty-five miles an hour.

'You were doing thirty-five.'

Meekly the driver confessed his sin.

'Let me see your licence.'

It was at home.

'What about the insurance.'

It was at home.

Fearing lest he might ask to see my letters of ordination or the crematorium certificate I felt that I had better forestall him.

'Officer', I spoke, 'Do you know that it is an offence in this country to interfere with divine service? We have just completed the first part and we are now, in suitably framed minds, proceeding to complete our mission at the crematorium. If you persist in further delaying us then I will be obliged to report you to your superiors.'

The serpent was effectively exorcised. On my return home,

without Dora or summons, I found the Vicarage had been burgled!

Retirement

Wild Cat

The sun set early as the hills were high but its golden store touched and gilded the tops of Drummond Hill across the plain from the hotel. The daylight lingered; indeed it never yielded completely to the night during July in this highland region. Our friends, Ron and Joan, joined us in our after-dinner walk to Glen Lyon. It was a comfortable hour, for then the midges seemed to remove their kicking boots or restrict their activities to twilight dancing under the bridge. Swallows seemed to have no curfew and mingled their flights with those of the nocturnal bats.

'It's great to be retired, Ron. While I'm kept very busy I don't have the responsibility. D'you know, this is the first holiday I've had for years when I've felt really and truly free; free from hourly expecting a recall for a funeral or a sickness or because a locum has let me down; free from having to think up sermons; free to choose when and where to go and how long to stay.'

We turned into the glen reputedly the loneliest, longest and loveliest glen in the Highlands. To our left the Black River tumbled in symphony down the Glen of Crooked Stones.

'Sssh! What's that over there?' whispered Ron.

'What? Where?' I whispered in return.

'Across that rough patch of grassland. What kind of creature is that?'

We all looked. Well away from us we could see in the uncertain light an object roughly eighteen inches high amidships with a curved and apparently hairy back and about

134

two feet in total length. None of us could identify it.

'Keep still', said Ron, 'It's coming towards us.'

I couldn't see it move, but decided to continue up the glen in order to look down on it. Its vagueness was not clarified by altitude, so I rejoined my companions.

'I think it's moved', said Ethel.

'No doubt about it', asserted Ron, 'It's come a good ten yards closer to us.'

It looked to be stationary to me.

Back in the hotel, where the licensing laws were apparently in abeyance, we recounted our encounter with the unknown beast. Rob was a huge highlander, articulate and wearing an aggressive and unruly beard which served as a sponge for the drops of wee drams the customers bought for him. He was a very learned man, an encyclopaedia of Scottish knowledge.

'Aye. I ken what ye hae' seen. Ne doot aboot it; a wildcat!' The proprietor wore the kilt.

'There are many up the glen and they hunt in the twilight. They're very vicious creatures and it's just as well you didn't disturb it, especially if it was stalking. Keep clear of them.' He's a sassenach.

For the next hour we were enthralled at the startling instructions given by Rob on the habits and life of wildcats.

Mr Turner, the proprietor, said, 'I have one that was made into a sporran. I'll go and fetch it for you. I got it cheap because it's cross-eyed!'

Sure enough, the maker of the sporran had succeeded in giving the wildcat an optical defect so that the eyes looked at one another. If, in real life, that wildcat had been afflicted with such a drawback it would no doubt have died of starvation or have bashed its brains out on the crags.

The sunshine warmed the east-facing front of the hotel when, after breakfast, Ethel and I went to the wee kirk for prayers. In the kirkyard stands the oldest living thing in Europe; a yew tree known to be at least four thousand years old.

'Let's go up the glen to see if we can catch a glimpse of our wildcat', suggested Ethel.

It was pleasant walking. The thatched cottages, havens for the birds, angled themselves neatly in picturesque rows. The 'death-stone' or 'plague-stone' pointed its shadow like a medieval sun-dial across the grass. We turned into the glen. The creature was still there. I began to worry in case it had been snared in a trap, while on the other hand I considered that it may have its 'nest' of kittens on the ground. Caution was the order of the moment as I crept slowly towards it.

Bathed and spruced up before dinner we propped ourselves beside the bar and the hulk of Rob, whose malt-scented whiskers pointed upwards towards the measures of spirits. Ron and Joan came in.

'Hey, Ron; had a good day? Been to the opticians?'

'Opticians? Why should I go there?'

'Remember that wildcat you saw last night creeping ten yards towards you?'

'Yes'

'Ethel and I have seen it today. It's a clump of thistles!'

What else would one expect at the birthplace of Pontius Pilate.

Sewer

Summer days, wildcats and procurators were just memories as I trudged through the frozen snow. Dai was a man after my own heart. There was so much in his life that reflected the path that I had trodden. His initials were JR. He had sailed the seven seas as a marine engineer serving under the 'red duster'. Like so many sea-going engineers he had seen the light in the engine room. Adjusting the telegraphs to 'full ahead' he had steered a theological course towards ordination. Still at full steam he began his ministry and with a blunt honesty and directness found among mariners he called a piston, a piston for he couldn't recognise a spade. He was Vicar of Sleekburn when I first met him. He answered my knocking on his front door in a cassock and a checked, cloth cap and said to me, a complete stranger,

'Howway in and sit down and keep quiet. I'm watching the test match'.

Elizabeth, his wife, gave me a cup of coffee to stifle any inclination to speak and without ascertaining if I imbibed, poured a generous measure of Lamb's Navy Rum into the beverage, which violated the plimsoll line and slopped into my saucer.

'Divvent waste it', said Dai, 'drink it from the saucer.'

Dai kept the flag flying at Mitford during the interregnum before I became incumbent. Elizabeth preserved him with wifely solicitations and rum but finally his blood-pressure broke the gauge, stopped engines and he joined the Big Fisherman at the harbour gates.

For ten years the snowdrops heralded spring time from Dai's grave. Snuggled before the dying embers of the fire, too tired to bother going to bed, my slumbering faculties were rudely awakened by the jangling of the phone. Having passed the ninety mark, Elizabeth had felt that she ought to see how Dai was faring in the New Jerusalem where there is no more sea. She said 'farewell' to Doreen and 'hello' to Dai and Doreen rang me.

A thick suede coat with woollen collar protected me from the cruel attacks of a sharp-pronged wind from the North Sea and Siberia. I shivered on the doorstep as I heard movements from the bowels of the house. I should have heeded the warning. Looking very much like her father, Doreen opened the hatch.

'Come in, Jack. It's lovely to see you. Good of you to come on a day like this.'

She conveyed me into the galley where I felt the gladdening warmth from the Rayburn stove and heard the sweet music of a kettle singing.

'Now it's coffee you take, and, if I remember rightly, no sugar.' I hoped that she would remember the other additive I usually supped and she did, for as she reached down the tin of coffee so her other hand wrapped around the navy rum.

'Make mine in a mug', I requested, not wishing to drink from the saucer.

'While I'm making the coffee, Jack, will you do me a favour?'

'Of course; I'll do anything for you.'

What a rash promise.

'The sewage is overflowing the manhole cover in the back yard. Will you clear it for me?'

'Can't you get the council to do it for you?'

'They can't come until tomorrow and the funeral is in the morning.'

Horribly reluctant, but a man of my word, I followed her into the concrete yard. The drain was overflowing, the stench like a casbah. Someone had cemented three sides of the manhole cover.

'Have you a chisel?'

'Somewhere, but I've never seen it since Dai passed on.'

Hoping that it would never be found I said,

'I can't do anything unless that cover is freed'. She found it.

My fingers were numb, my nose protested at the pervading pollution and my stomach began to revolt. I could not find suitable rods or implements to effect a clearance.

'Have you anything I can use to get into this slime?'

'I'm afraid not', said Doreen from the far-off doorway, 'You'll have to use your hand'.

I stripped to the waist. My veins stood out like a roadmap. I plunged deep into exploration and eventually cleared a channel through which the effluent gurgled slowly but surely.

Frozen to the marrow, with my senses mercifully numbed, I held my arm under the hot tap.

'Ready for your coffee now, Jack?' blithely enquired the delighted Doreen.

Later in the luxury of a bath, liberally clouded with Dettol I reflected that even retirement has its stirring moments.

A Grave Matter

'Can you consecrate a grave for me?'
Bob's voice was urgent yet discreetly confidential over the
phone.
'Going to die soon, then. Picked your plot already?' I replied.
'No, no, not mine. I don't want to get into your clutches yet.
I'd like to see you away first. Seriously Jack, will you do it as a
favour to me?'
'Where is it? In your back garden?'
'Of course not. Be serious.'
'Okay, is it in a cemetery or churchyard that has not been
fully consecrated?'
'No, nothing like that. I wish it was.'
Lapsing into my amused and interested puzzlement I
enquired,
'You haven't been polishing anyone off, have you?'
'Not me; but someone else may have done, and I know where
the body is buried.'
'Where?'
'At the riverside near Riding Mill', said Bob in an almost
undiscernable whisper.
'Just a minute. Hang on, there. Let's just get this straight.

You are serious, Bob, and I think you may be referring to the murder trial that's just been adjourned.'
'Yes.'

A man had been accused of the murder of his wife ten years previously. He had allegedly confessed to the crime now and had taken the police to a site on the banks of the river Tyne where he claimed to have buried her body. The trial had been adjourned indefinitely because of the distressed mind of the accused.

'Well, the police have been up the river and for over a space of three weeks have dug where the man indicated but have found no body', I protested.

'Aye, that's right. But they've been digging in the wrong place.'

'How do you know?'

'I saw him ten years ago burying his wife. Her body is half a mile further down the bank.'

'If you are right then there is only one course for you to take, Bob, go to the police and tell them.'

'I've been twice. They don't seem to be particularly interested. I've heard nothing from them since I reported it. So if the body is going to remain there, would you consecrate the grave? I don't like to think that she's lying there in unconsecrated ground.'

'Well, Bob, tell me all about it; how you know and what you actually saw.'

'That's easy because at the time I entered it into my diary; date, time and happening.'

In that vicinity in pursuance of his work he had seen a car pull up near to the riverside.

'A man got out of the car, took out a spade and walked to the river bank where he was obscured from my view by shrubs. After a while he came back to the car. He opened the boot and took out what at first appeared to me to be a roll of carpet, which he carried to the water's edge. I got a clearer view and it looked very much as if his burden was a clothed, woman's body. Later he returned to the car carrying only the spade. He then drove away.'

'What did you do then?' I asked.

'I went to see what he had dug. The disturbed area was about five feet square, not the average six feet by three of a grave. So I concluded it must have been rubbish he had buried.'

'Did you tell anyone about this?'

'No. But I entered it into my diary and kept an eye on the newspapers to see if anyone was reported as missing, but drew a blank'.

'Why have you come forward now?'

'This murder case has brought it all back to me, especially with the police digging in that area. I'm sure that the man was burying a woman.'

'Well, Bob, there's only one thing that I can do. With your permission I'll go to the police.'

I told the story to the Chief Superintendent and the Detective Inspector. They acted. Together with Bob and a team of police they went to the site which Bob suggested was the correct site of the burial. Unfortunately the river was in flood, well above the line of the alleged grave. The river remained in spate for several weeks and the trial was resumed.

The defending counsel contacted me. Could he come out to see me? That evening he arrived. I signed a statement detailing all that I had been told.

Then the counsel asked me,

'Is he a man of fantasies? Is he given to dreaming or fantasising? Does he like publicity?'

I could honestly answer that Bob was realistic, down to earth; a matter of fact person. Contrary to seeking publicity he is a quiet, retiring type.

'Didn't his diary show that he'd seen something? He wrote it ten years before this case.'

The following day the counsel rang me again.

'There are a couple of points I need you to clarify. Can I come along tomorrow about four?'

That evening the newspaper reported that it was likely that the jury and judge would visit the riverside and that the judge had recommended that the jurors wear wellington boots.

The drama ended suddenly. The counsel rang me at lunch time.

'Thank you very much, Reverend Richardson, for agreeing to see me this evening, but I shall not be coming. It's all over. The Judge has instructed the jury to acquit the accused.'

So, if there is a grave, it remains unconsecrated; until I get another phone call.

Epilogue

The trees sketched the sunlight into multitudinous designs which entranced me as the soft, warm breeze moved the patterns into a dancing kaleidoscope. Two young fawns, absolutely stationary, watched me from a safe distance in the woods. My foot snapped a dry twig and the deer vanished more quickly than the sound as a rabbit shot across my path.

Blagdon's beauty is my privilege. Here among the cows, pheasants, squirrels and nature's variety from frogs to ferrets, I spend my retirement. This is a period of new beginnings. We begin, I suppose, when we are conceived and yet again when we are delivered from the dark entombment of the womb. Childhood begins after babyhood. We begin the pressure game at school. Our instincts and emotions steer us to new relationships in our adolescence. Manhood, marriage and parenthood lead us in swift procession from one beginning to another. Work opens up new horizons. We begin anew, recollecting our past parental responsibilities, with the joy of grandparenthood and so in the chain of beginning and end we reach the link which is erroneously called 'retirement'.

At Nick's Bridge in Blagdon Wood I watched a dragonfly, newly flighted; its bright blue pencil hovering as if in an artist's hand over a canvas of greens, as its wings beat the air into a supporting cushion. Suddenly it was away beneath the bridge and from my breath-holding gaze. The rough chips on the road leading to the hog-backed bridge at Belasis, the smoother turnpike, the muddy yet sky-reflecting patches near the oddly-named Make Me Rich and the gentle slope home united in a parable of life. Each turn a new vista as in the changing scenes of life; each surface a replica of life's rough and smooth; the rain pools causing me to choose carefully my path and to pause and, like them, reflect.

So I'll walk at one with God, neighbour and nature until when walking days are done, I will begin again where there is no ending.

In the meantime I will keep my diary and, in God's mercy, a twinkle in my eye.